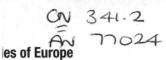

...es of Europe

www.leftrepublican.com is an independent political platform
bringing together left, republican, feminist and green voices from
across Ireland in a spirit of open debate and dialogue. We aim
to provide space for all shades of progressive opinion in Ireland
and to provoke discussion on political, economic, strategic and
organisational issues. We also aim to provide a platform for those
forces and voices from across the globe who are struggling for
independence, socialism, democracy and peace.

The Transnational Institute is an independent fellowship of
researchers and activists living in different parts of the world,
who develop innovative analyses of world affairs. It serves no
government, political party or interest group.

We the Peoples of Europe

Susan George

Pluto Press
LONDON • ANN ARBOR, MI

First published 2008 by Pluto Press
345 Archway Road, London N6 5AA
and 839 Greene Street, Ann Arbor, MI 48106

www.plutobooks.com

www.tni.org/george

British Library Cataloguing in Publication Data
A catalogue record for this book is available from the British Library

ISBN   978 0 7453 2634 4   Hardback
ISBN   978 0 7453 2633 7   Paperback

Library of Congress Cataloging in Publication Data applied for

This book is printed on paper suitable for recycling and made from
fully managed and sustained forest sources. Logging, pulping and
manufacturing processes are expected to conform to the environmental
regulations of the country of origin.

10   9   8   7   6   5   4   3   2   1

Designed and produced for Pluto Press by
Chase Publishing Services Ltd, Sidmouth, EX10 9QG, England
Typeset from disk by Stanford DTP Services, Northampton, England
Printed and bound in the European Union by
CPI Antony Rowe Ltd, Chippenham and Eastbourne, England

Contents

Foreword

Robert Ballagh

Let me say straight away that, in my opinion, there is nothing more disquieting than the feeling of being railroaded into something.

For example, many years ago, I remember being trapped by a zealous time-share salesman in the south of Spain and, as a consequence, experiencing unease trying to escape from his over-eager attempt to sell me something that I didn't want.

The unrelenting way the European elites have pursued their objectives has, for me, provoked similar feelings of discomfort and certainly a hankering to question their motives.

Without doubt their unwillingness to take no for an answer mirrors the practice of the high pressure salesman, and certainly we, in Ireland, have recent memories of such bullying behaviour. After we had the temerity to vote no to the Nice Treaty we were simply sent back to vote again and told to come back with the "right" answer the next time!

Sadly the Irish are not alone in having their democratic decisions ignored by the elites who run Europe. When France and Holland voted against the EU Constitution one would have presumed that their proposed document, as a consequence, would have become null and void, since ratification required unanimous support by all EU member states. However, rather than accepting the democratic decision of both the French and the Dutch, the European elites decided instead to plough ahead with the rejected document. Their tactic was to convert it into another document by simply altering its name and by making minimal cosmetic changes to its content.

Certainly many politicians are of the view that little has changed. Irish Taoiseach, Bertie Ahern remarked that "90 per cent of it is still there", while Irish Foreign Minister, Dermot Ahern said that "the substance of what was agreed in 2004 has been retained. What is gone is the term – Constitution."

In my opinion, this comment is of particular significance for as Giuliano Amato, the former Italian Prime Minister said at the London School of Economics, "the good thing about not calling it a Constitution is that no one can call for a referendum on it". And sadly this undemocratic option has become a political reality.

With the exception of Ireland not one referendum will be held in Europe to decide on this fundamental treaty, that if ratified, will impact on all the citizens of Europe.

By the way, Irish citizens only have a constitutional right to vote by referendum on issues like EU treaties, because of the legal case taken by that great Irish patriot Raymond Crotty. Worryingly, however, if this Lisbon Treaty is carried, that democratic right will disappear as the new treaty will not require any future amendment to be approved by referendum. Without doubt, the European elites are both contemptuous of and irritated by any involvement by the peoples of Europe in the decision making process.

For example, President Nicolas Sarkozy of France admitted that "France was just ahead of all the other countries in voting no, it would happen in all member states if they have a referendum, there is a cleavage between people and governments and a referendum now would bring Europe into danger. There will be no treaty if we have a referendum in France", while ex-Irish Taoiseach Dr Garrett Fitzgerald ruefully observed that "the changes [between the failed EU Constitution and the Lisbon Treaty] have simply been designed to enable heads of government to sell to their people the idea of ratification by parliamentary action rather than referendum". Finally, Commission President José Manuel Barroso confessed that "referendums make the process of approval of European treaties much more complicated and less predictable... it makes *our* lives, with 27 member states in the EU, much more difficult".

I should, I guess, at this stage confess that right from the start I have been a Euro sceptic. Well, perhaps not quite "right from the start", for in 1951, when France and Germany merged the management of their coal and steel industries, which set in train what was to become the "common market", I was still in short trousers and probably playing Cowboys and Indians with my pals!

However as soon as I was old enough, and especially when Ireland became involved in what was then called the "European Economic Community", I began to question the nature of this particular European project and where it was headed.

As a consequence of such deliberations I found myself campaigning against the various treaties that required ratification and I have to say that adopting this oppositional role in Ireland, at that time, proved to be neither popular nor profitable. Because of the policy adopted by the EEC of helping the poorer countries (Portugal, Ireland, Greece and Spain) to catch up with the wealthier countries through large transfers of wealth, few in Ireland were prepared to ask any fundamental questions about the European project.

In fact most people in Ireland seemed quite content to simply cash the cheques from Bruxelles whilst at the same time pinning their faith on the notion that there is such a thing as a free lunch.

Of course, right from the start, there have been many serious issues worthy of discussion and debate, and, in my opinion, one example of major concern is the democratic deficit that lies at the heart of this European project.

This is demonstrated by the fact that the Commission, an unelected, opaque and unaccountable body, holds practically all executive, legislative and judicial power whilst at the same time, the parliament, the only part of the European superstructure actually elected by the peoples of Europe, is no more than an expensive toothless talking shop. By the way, the proposed Lisbon Treaty does nothing to challenge this democratic deficit; in fact, the powers of the Commission will be enhanced if the treaty comes into force.

Many times over the last 30 years I have heard concerned citizens attempt to raise uncomfortable questions about the European project only to be dismissed as negative and irrelevant.

For example, I remember a public meeting where Raymond Crotty warned that the full implementation of the common agricultural policy would signal the end of the small family farm in Ireland. Well, he was booed,

We the Peoples of Europe

jeered, called a fantasist and even worse, mad; yet today, no one can deny that the future is truly bleak for the small farmer in Ireland.

For many years there seemed to be a pathological resistance to any real debate about Europe on the grounds that any negative rumblings might derail the gravy train that regularly set out from Bruxelles. Nowadays, of course, the departures are less frequent and carry less freight, and soon there may be no trains at all!

These realities are slowly changing attitudes to the European project in Ireland and many who were unquestioning supporters in the past are now beginning to wonder about the project and where it is heading; especially those who have been negatively affected by EU policy, for example, sugar beet farmers, fishermen and the parents of primary school children who find they are now being tasked with the payment of huge water bills!

One of the persistent accusations levelled against those who are sceptical about certain aspects of the European project is that they are, in essence, anti-European – or even worse, narrow minded xenophobes! Speaking for myself nothing could be further from the truth.

Some time ago I visited southern India and marvelled before the immense *gopurams* or entrance towers to the Meenakshi temple in Madurai. I found myself awe-struck by the exotic beauty of the polychrome carvings of Hindu deities which adorned these mysterious structures, but I must confess that my wonderment was that of a stranger, intense but essentially superficial.

On the other hand when I enter, say, the gothic cathedral in Amiens, once again I feel a similar sense of awe but also, and more importantly, a sense of connectedness. This is because the cathedral is not just a magnificent structure, but is, at the same time, a manifestation of European culture, a culture to which I belong.

On a trip to Japan some time ago my hosts brought me to the Kabuki theatre in Tokyo, where I was both astonished and dazzled by the experience, but I have to acknowledge that I had little or no understanding of what it was about. Of course the same is not true when I see a play by, say, Ibsen or Wilde. The obvious reason is that these great playwrights wrote out of their European experience, an experience that I share.

These are the kind of cultural achievements that represent the Europe that I celebrate and feel part of, a Europe that forged a culture, an identity and a social model found nowhere else on the globe. Centuries of struggle have produced structures that balance rights with responsibilities, and that encourage the formation of a social model that takes responsibility for the poor, the sick and the oppressed.

Yet it seems to me that this existing European social and cultural model is under constant threat from what I see as alien value systems. And to my mind the latest and most pernicious threat is the proposed Lisbon Treaty.

The most obvious aspect of the treaty is its sheer physical bulk, consisting of hundreds of pages of dense prose which make comprehension difficult if not impossible.

Now, this is not an accident. I believe that the treaty has been drafted in such a manner in order to exclude the ordinary citizen; after all, the Belgian Foreign Minister Karel de Gucht admitted that "the aim of this treaty is to be unreadable... to be unclear. It is a success."

As Susan George notes, "those who govern us use the well-honed tool of complexity. Texts which have an impact on our work, our rights and our lives, are increasingly indecipherable", and I believe that one unfortunate and possibly deliberate consequence of this is that many citizens fall into apathy or despair, and unconsciously allow others to assume control. From the point of view of the European elites, confusion can yield quite satisfactory results!

If you manage to get your hands on a copy of the Lisbon Treaty (as I write copies are as scarce as hen's teeth) and are prepared to wade into its dense political text and examine the grammar of its composition, then very quickly you will begin to unearth a definite bias.

Anywhere the treaty deals with issues such as the internal market, the free movement of goods, competition policy and so on, the verbs used in the text are clear, unambiguous and affirmative – verbs like "shall do", "will comply" and "must enforce". On the other hand, when the treaty refers to issues like the rights of citizens it collapses into the subjunctive with verbs like "hopes to" and "aims at", as in "aiming at full employment and social progress". Well, as Susan George puts it, "one can 'aim at' anything for years without necessarily reaching the target".

Most enthusiastic advocates of the Lisbon Treaty insist that it is necessary in order to make the EU more effective and more efficient. In a sense this may be true, but it begs the question: more effective and more efficient for whom, and at what price?

It seems to me that the Lisbon Treaty slavishly follows the Americanised neo-liberal economic model, where belief in the competitive free market is paramount.

Undoubtedly this model benefits establishment interests, large corporations and those who thrive in a free market situation, but neo-liberal policies certainly do not defend the poor, the weak and the disadvantaged, and the growing inequality gap anywhere such policies prevail is there to prove it.

The Lisbon Treaty is, in essence, a manual for running an economy; therefore, as a consequence, it provides scant social protection for the citizens of Europe.

We are at a crossroads at present but the referendum in Ireland can provide us with a unique opportunity to choose in which direction we wish to travel.

We can vote for an Americanised, competitive, "survival of the fittest" type of Europe or we can seek to defend the existing but threatened European social model which continues to balance rights with responsibilities.

As an Irish citizen with a keen interest in Irish society I have to admit that I am deeply concerned by the impact that a ratified Lisbon Treaty will have on Irish sovereignty. Now I am well aware that one cost of our membership of the European Union has been the steady erosion of our sovereignty through the ratification of various treaties, for example Maastricht and Nice; however the ratification of the Lisbon Treaty will mark a radical shift in the relationship between the European Union and its member states.

To understand the extent of this shift one needs to appreciate that what we call the European Union today is not a state. It is not even a legal or corporate entity in its own right; however a successful Lisbon Treaty will establish a legally quite new European Union. This will be a Union in the constitutional form of a supranational European state. The European Union of which our countries are all

We the Peoples of Europe

currently members will cease to exist and will be replaced by this legally new European Union which will be separate from and superior to its member states, just as the USA is separate from and superior to say Kansas or Louisiana.

By transforming the legal character of the Union the Lisbon Treaty will transform the meaning of Union citizenship. Presently, each and every one of us is, firstly, a citizen of our own country (in our case, Ireland) and then a member of the European Union. If the Lisbon Treaty is ratified each person will become, firstly, a citizen of Europe and secondly a citizen of Ireland. The rights and duties attaching to this citizenship of the new Union will be superior to those attaching to citizenship of one's own national state, and even though member states will retain their own national constitutions these will be subordinate to the new Union Treaty regulations. As such they will no longer be constitutions of sovereign states in their own right, but instead will resemble the constitutions of various local states in the USA which, of course, are subordinate to the federal US constitution.

To put it simply and directly, if the Lisbon Treaty is passed then a sovereign independent Irish nation will no longer exist. Considering our history I am astonished that we are even contemplating such a profound outcome. The dream of an Ireland where Irish people would have control over their own destinies was what fuelled the centuries of struggle carried out by Theobold Wolfe Tone, Robert Emmet, Daniel O'Connell, Charles Stuart Parnell, Patrick Pearse and James Connolly.

The loss of national sovereignty implicit in the Lisbon Treaty will represent a renunciation of those centuries of struggle!

For some time now I have been puzzled by the fact that most people in positions of power and influence in Ireland have been unswerving and uncritical cheerleaders for the European project, this in spite of the fact that not every single decision by the EU has favoured Ireland.

Now, I accept that those who individually benefit from membership of the EU will naturally be keen supporters, and I specifically refer to large businesses and corporations who continually seek unfettered opportunities to maximise profit, and I'm pretty sure that the recent decision by the European Court to find against a Swedish trade union that had campaigned for the rights of Latvian migrant workers in Sweden would have pleased those corporate interests; but I wonder if there were others who might have recognised Americanised neo-liberal strategies at work here, strategies that are currently infecting this European project. Unfortunately, it seems that in spite of this worrying development, many politicians, trade unionists and journalists who claim to represent non-corporate interests, still continue to support this European project, or at best remain mute.

Could the reason for the almost unanimous and uncritical support for the European Union by the Irish establishment be symptomatic of a profound lack of vision? It seems to me that for a long time now Ireland has been intellectually adrift and rudderless.

The political leadership of the country seems to have no particular idea about the country, what it stands for or where it is going.

So it seems to me that what they did was what any person without ideas or vision would do; they hitched a lift from someone who was not only confident but knew exactly where they were going!

In our case this was the European project which, right from the start, has been driven by people who knew precisely what they were doing.

In the words of ex-Commission President Romano Prodi, "Are we all clear that we want to build something that can aspire to be a world power? In other words not just a trading block, but a political entity."

So for the visionless Irish this proved to be the perfect solution, simply join up with others who will do your thinking for you!

Well, ironically, the time has arrived when we, the Irish, will have to do our own thinking and not just for us but for all of Europe.

The Lisbon Treaty presents us with a stark choice.

Do we want an undemocratic supranational state that will subvert Irish sovereignty and be run according to an Americanised neo-liberal model, or do we want to defend a Europe consisting of a cooperative assembly of nations operating a social model that is the envy of the world?

The choice is ours however, and make no mistake about it, those who choose to campaign against the Lisbon Treaty will be subjected to powerful negative abuse; in fact it has started already. Commissioner Charlie McCreevy is on record as saying that if the Irish vote against the treaty we will be seen as the laughing stock of Europe, and Taoiseach Bertie Ahern said that a negative vote would result in Ireland being cut adrift from the rest of Europe. I would suggest that such remarks qualify as scaremongering rather than rational debate.

Nonetheless, I remain convinced that if the Irish people vote against the Lisbon Treaty, they will be striking a blow for democracy and, at the same time, will demonstrate their solidarity with their fellow Europeans who, on this occasion, have been denied their democratic rights.

A No vote will also force the EU's Prime Ministers and Presidents to go back and think again, and to consult with their populations before they come up with a new document which, this time, must respect the will of the peoples of Europe.

About Robert Ballagh

Robert Ballagh is an Irish artist. He was born in Dublin and graduated from the Dublin Institute of Technology. He is both a painter and designer. His painting style was strongly influenced by pop art and his paintings are often playful and didactic.

In 1991, he coordinated the 75th anniversary commemoration of the 1916 Easter Rising. Interviewed for a special feature that was published in the *Irish Times* on the 90th anniversary, he related that this had caused him to be harassed by the Special Branch of the Garda Siochána.

Ballagh represented Ireland at the 1969 Paris Biennale. Among the theatre sets he has designed are sets for *Riverdance*, Samuel Beckett's *Endgame* (1991) and Oscar Wilde's *Salomé* (1998). He has also designed over 70 Irish postage stamps and the last series of Irish banknotes, "Series C", before the introduction of the euro. He is a member of Aosdána.

Robert Ballagh has been actively involved in radical Irish politics for over 30 years.

Introduction

Introductions are often best written when the rest of the work has been completed. As I revisit this one at the end of a long road, let me introduce something new into the introduction, an unfolding European story.

It sounds technical, even boring – indeed what could be more boring than financial accounting – but it's not. It tells us a great deal about European politics and our own individual futures, including what level of taxes we will pay and what services, healthcare, education and so on we will enjoy. Here is the plot summary: In 2001, a private group set up the very official-sounding International Accounting Standards Board (IASB). The people involved came mostly from the Big Four worldwide accounting firms – Deloitte, Ernst & Young, KPMG, PricewaterhouseCoopers – or from transnational corporations (TNCs) and banks. They incorporated their new non-profit organisation in the US state of Delaware, the most corporate-friendly of the 50 US states and, although there was nothing official about them and their new organisation, their aim seemed clear and comprehensible, even laudable. You can't have a global economy with dozens of different accounting systems so you must try to get governments to agree on commonly accepted standards.

Fair enough. Europe alone had over two dozen systems and wanted to become a big international player for inward and outward foreign investment. As the Chairman of the IASB, Scottish chartered accountant Sir David Tweedie put it in a declaration to the United States Senate in October 2007, "the lack of a common, well-respected financial reporting language in Europe was an impediment to economic growth and the development of capital markets to rival other areas of the world".

Was the self-appointed International Accounting Standards Board merely an expression of wishful thinking on the part of transnational accounting firms? Curiously enough, immediately after its incorporation, the European Commission passed legislation requiring that by 2005, IASB standards be applied by all European companies listed on all European stock exchanges. For those who understood what was going on, this decision raised unwelcome questions: Should a self-appointed, private body emanating from firms with an obvious interest in tailoring standards to their own needs be making hard public-interest law, by itself? What kinds of standards, exactly, apply in the 100-some countries that now adhere or soon will adhere to IASB prescriptions? What will corporations have to report and what can they keep secret? Should parliaments and civil society organisations and experts be allowed to participate in the debates concerning the development, implementation and monitoring of standards?

Many people, particularly accountants and tax specialists in Europe who were aware of the changes taking place, thought they had the right to comment. They believed in particular that the European Commissioner for the Internal Market, the hard-line neo-liberal Irishman Charlie McCreevy (himself a chartered accountant), should not be working directly with the IASB without appropriate scrutiny and be permitted to push through whatever standards he liked. The Commission nonetheless issued directives making the IASB standards the law of the land, with no democratic process or oversight whatsoever.

The Tax Justice Network (TJN) has considered submitting the accounts of a major transnational corporation to the Booker Prize Committee on the grounds that they constitute a work of fiction. Indeed, as the TJN's own chartered accountant expert Richard Murphy puts it, "all transnational corporation accounts are fictional". But fiction can be more or less true to life, and accounts would be much more so if TNCs were required to disclose what their revenues (or losses) and profits have been in each national jurisdiction where they operate.

The IASB, instead, provides an enormous loophole through which you can propel innumerable container-ships, aeroplanes and trucks. Companies need not say where their real business activity actually takes place. This is the perfect cover for "transfer pricing", the method universally used through which a company buys and sells from itself, at whatever price it may choose, so as to diminish its real revenues and profits in high-tax countries and increase them in low- or no-tax jurisdictions. Over half of all world trade now consists in intra-firm trade (BP "trading" with BP, IBM with IBM, and so on) so we are talking extremely large sums of money. If companies had to report on the basis of national jurisdictions where they operate, citizens and investors might find it a bit fishy if company X reported large sales and profits in, say, the Cayman Islands where its presence amounted to a brass plate on a door and very poor results in, say, France or Germany where it employed hundreds. But the curious have no opportunity to identify the fish-factor because of the way accounts can now be legally presented.

In 2006, an NGO network began lobbying for country-by-country reporting and the European Parliament finally got a belated chance to review McCreevy's and the IASB's proposals. The Parliament eventually said OK, but with so many caveats and observations that it amounted to a requirement for review; it also joined NGOs in demanding the country-by-country principle, at least for the "extractive industries" (mines and oil). Eighty civil society commentators weighed in to support this demand. The IASB countered by getting eighty of its own buddies to support their non-geographical system. Then civil society got the matter into the *Financial Times*, which experienced a "Hey, wait a minute" moment, correctly observing that investors too needed that information. If they didn't have it, and as a result made bad decisions, the longer-term result would be to increase the cost of capital, clearly anathema to the *FT*.

The story is much longer than this, I'm only touching the highlights, and it's not over yet. But it illustrates some essential points which will concern us throughout this book:

- Do we want a Europe of 480 million citizens in which one unelected Commissioner is in effect able to make official law, the latter drafted by private interest groups emanating from the world of high finance and transnational business?
- Do we want a Europe in which the peoples' representatives in Parliament are obliged to fight every step of the way to be able even to review – not change, *review* – a Commission decision?

- Do we want a Europe in which privately made "hard" law will make it forever impossible to tax at true and fair rates transnational corporations in national jurisdictions?
- If corporations are not paying their fair share of taxes – and all the official figures show that their share is indeed declining in national accounts – do we accept that purely national business and citizens pay the shortfall in their stead, simply because they have a fixed address and no way of dissimulating their payrolls, incomes, consumption, etc.?
- Similarly, are we willing to forgo the services that corporate taxes might have paid for, had they been fairly assessed, or, as above, pay for them by ourselves?
- Do we find it normal that a matter so important for the future is pushed through with no debate, because it can be made to seem technical, boring and altogether impenetrable for the ordinary citizen?

These questions all come down to asking if people, if democracy, have any role to play in the new Europe, or if we should simply accept that our futures will henceforward be determined by an elite minority. And this brings me to the heart of this book, *We the Peoples of Europe*.

During the spring of 2005, France witnessed a debate and a positive political outcome unequalled in decades. The victory of the "No" in the referendum on the Constitutional Treaty was a victory for the Europe of the future and for the human spirit, in the best Enlightenment tradition. For me, as for millions of other French men and women, the evening of 29 May was a joyful occasion. Despite the official stance of most parties and some unions, despite an unprecedented media bombardment in favour of the "Yes", the French stood tall and refused to accept an unacceptable text. I admit I gave way to full lyrical mode when I heard the results. It seemed to me then that those looking back to 2005 fifty or a hundred years from now would recognise it as a turning point not only in the direction of Europe but as an important chapter in the history of human emancipation.

I wrote the book you have in hand, in French, during and after that campaign and that victory; it was published in France and in Spain and I thought that was the end of it. Now, however, it is late October 2007. Despite the French and Dutch rejections of the Constitutional Treaty a year and a half ago, it has boomeranged back and hit Europeans full in the face: the boomerang is called the "Reform" Treaty. It is nothing of the kind, and we shall soon see why, but the subject has again become topical and I've been asked to rewrite what is now *We the Peoples of Europe* in my mother-tongue. Frankly, I tried to avoid this job, but faced with an eminently clunky, frequently inaccurate translation by somebody else, I recognised that I had to do it – if only because history had marched on and one couldn't ask a translator – even a bad one – to replace the initial author for providing updates.

I love and respect both my languages and try to be worthy of them when I write, but I hate to translate because getting the tone right when I shift from one to the other is so beastly difficult. So I haven't "translated" – I have rewritten – and am now glad to have made the effort. I shall be gladder still if the Irish vote No in their obligatory, statutory referendum or if the British manage to obtain one, but even if they don't,

We the Peoples of Europe

I shall at least have explained to some people the importance of what I believe to be at stake.

As the reader will discover, I've merged past and present, combining the 2005 *Nous Peuples d'Europe* about the Constitutional Treaty with the debate over the Reform Treaty that is its reincarnation. I tell the story of the earlier debate and referendum pretty much as I told it in French two years ago, although I've cut some parts that took aim at certain politicians who are of scant interest outside – perhaps even inside – France. In Chapter 3, I also compare the Treaty on European desks at this moment with the one we rejected, showing that it's as if we had never voted. From Chapter 3 to the end, I elaborate on the Europe I think we should strive to create. We have very little time.

Now let's rewind to 2005. Although I may well have been mistaken about the historical importance of the French vote rejecting the Constitution, it was crucial at the time and because that achievement still stands as a milestone, it deserves praise. We had to curb the onslaught of neo-liberalism and the referendum campaign did that, at least for a time.

The financial, political and media elites in favour of the "Yes" were furious. They reacted like wounded beasts, yapping and biting and making constant attacks against the progressive forces of the "No", guilty as charged of all known sins against society and sanity. But even these elites, with all the means at their disposal, couldn't convince the French that they had participated – or at least 70 per cent of them had participated – in an anti-European vote. Even our worst enemies eventually had to admit that of the 55 per cent of voters who opted for the No, at most 17–18 per cent were genuinely "souverainistes" (French "sovereigntists" of left or right) or anti-European rightwing nationalists, or against the idea that Turkey might one day join the EU. For everyone else, it was not an "anti" but an "alter"-European vote, in the same sense that as we say "alter-mondialiste" or "alter-globalist". We wanted then and we still want now a different, humane, democratic, social Europe – not the neo-liberal caricature the Constitution promised to foist upon us.

After the triumph of the "No", the French political class turned its attention to reshuffling the national political cards in view of the 2007 presidential and parliamentary elections. The one thing all of them and all the parties seemed to agree on then was that you could not make the French vote again on the same text – or worse, try to force it through – without causing a full-scale revolution. Yet now they have done exactly that. They've reshuffled the Constitution as well and called it something else, to make it, as Valéry Giscard d'Estaing said, "easier to swallow". We were wrong to believe that the victory of the No and the impotent rage of the right might be the beginning of the end of their reign but when Nicolas Sarkozy won the presidency, it became clear this was not to be.

Let me put my authorial cards on the table now. I was born in the United States but have lived in France for decades and have become a French citizen. I have never belonged to any political party. My personal allegiance in France is to social movements like Attac,* which is not a party and has no intention of becoming one; it refuses on

* Association for the Taxation of Financial Transactions to Aid Citizens. Founded in 1998 around the idea of what we then called the "Tobin Tax", the agenda has broadened and encompasses the national, European and international aspects of neo-liberalism.

principle to endorse any candidate for any office. Attac has over 200 local committees in France and it was recognised everywhere as an extremely important component of the victory of the No. There are Attacs now in most European countries, in Japan and several Latin American countries but not in Britain or Ireland (or in the United States for that matter; there is a small one in Australia though).

As explained above, I wrote this during and after the campaign and it was published by my usual French publisher, Fayard, in September 2005. I saw the book then – and still do – as prolonging the campaign itself and as my contribution to continuing Attac's political work. My goal was to broaden the scope of the debate because I felt that the French and the Dutch, by voting No, had taken on responsibilities extending way beyond their national boundaries. Throughout Europe and indeed elsewhere, the French vote was observed and commented upon, approved and disapproved, understood and misunderstood; it aroused hope, jubilation, suspicion, hostility and a range of sentiments in between.

In France, the referendum victory of 2005 was followed in 2006 by a successful campaign against the CPE (Contrat de premier emploi, or First Employment Contract) which provoked massive street demonstrations until it was withdrawn. Then in 2007, the progressive forces adroitly – and alas typically – snatched defeat from the jaws of victory. That sad story is not the one I will tell here; I propose rather that we look at the meaning of the proposed, defeated, Constitution in historical perspective and see what it might mean for the future, particularly in the light of the right's renewed vigour and the new "Reform" Treaty.

The Constitution was a machine for casting Europe firmly in the United States mould and this is the main reason why refusing it was historic. I believe that Europe, for the time being at least, is the only political entity in the world that could – stressing the conditional *could* – offer an alternative model to the ultra-liberal model of the US or to China's totalitarian, workaholic one combining the worst features of both capitalism and communism. Remarkably encouraging developments are taking place in Latin America and in scattered places elsewhere but the European social model – imperfect as it may be, under threat as it surely is – remains the world's longest-standing contemporary political triumph of improved living standards for ordinary people, human ingenuity, tenacity and emancipation.

For that reason (as well as for other, geopolitical ones) we should assume that both the United States and China will oppose further democratic development in Europe and the emergence of a united front of 450 million people (perhaps more) enjoying a high GNP, excellent educational levels, healthcare provision, leading-edge research capacity and outstanding public services. If the progressive forces that campaigned for the "No" had their way; if they were able to shape Europe to their ideal, it would be unique. It would be home to efficient, integrated, inexpensive or free public services, a full-employment, ecological economy based on the preservation and enhancement of the planet and the satisfaction of human needs, a capacity for united social and political action, lifelong education and many other benefits for its citizens.

This is admittedly a vision, but it need not be utopian. To achieve it, Europe must overcome several obstacles. First, it must free itself from the hold of an increasingly neo-liberal economic regime established and fortified by successive EU treaties. These now almost exclusively benefit Establishment interests, large corporations and those who thrive on free market competition and who are, not coincidentally, already best-off. Neo-liberal policies most certainly do not defend the poor, the weak, the handicapped, the less well educated. The growing inequality gap in Europe (as in the rest of the world) is there to prove it. The public space and common-good dimensions of society are fast disappearing and sometimes seem all but lost.

If French and Dutch No voters and European progressives in general want the peoples of Europe to be well served; to preserve a significant public space, an environmental model and a humane economy, then we who spent months campaigning against a text that would have eradicated them all must now work to bring these goals to the fore. We must listen to the citizens of all European countries, share our experience with them, explain our vote and try to persuade them that we chose the right course. This implies a debate which recognises the very different levels of knowledge about European institutions and the texts that govern them, takes into account different visions of the future and acknowledges the unique perspective of each country. This will be the key to our success.

During the months preceding the referendum of 29 May 2005, France was gripped by a kind of mass happening, the scene of one of the most formidable debates I ever witnessed, equalled only by the one of that other, long-gone May forty years ago. Passion, reason, knowledge, analysis, interpretation, energy, engagement – all the vital ingredients were there. Our enthusiasm stood in sharp contrast to the status quo in many other European countries where people simply accepted the vague notion of "Europe" as A Good Thing. No particular debate seemed required and governments not only encouraged but expected an uncritical approach on the part of their citizens. People often knew virtually nothing about the actual content of European texts, particularly the one about to take precedence over their own national constitutions. The mainstream view came down to something like "The market, given time, will make us all rich. The Americans are our allies and NATO protects us. The construction of the European Union must continue to advance; never mind how. The text may not be perfect but it's the best we're going to get. All is for the best in the best of all possible Europes." Governments, always happier when the people are more or less anaesthetised, had no intention of awakening them.

The French No camp and other progressives need to understand that most of our European neighbours were kept completely in the dark about the Constitution and were denied referenda, indeed any discussion at all. In Germany and Italy, it was virtually impossible to obtain so much as a copy of the text in the local language, whereas in France, the immensely long, abstruse and boring text was at the top of the bestseller list, surely a first for La Documentation Française, the official agency that published it. Most Europeans saw ratification by parliamentary vote as a mere formality. Consequently, we need to explain why the French debate was so intense and why, at least back in May 2005, it seemed to us that the French vote had changed our common future as Europeans.

To rise above such a depressing level of awareness, we – I am talking about the French – have to listen to other Europeans and accept their criticism while still defending the rightness of the French vote against the Constitution. Some of my European, non-French friends (including the francophiles) were completely nonplussed by the French vote, often seen abroad as a victory for the right, not the left; a view relentlessly encouraged by their own media. Countries like Spain, Greece or Portugal, governed by dictators for decades before they joined the EU, had a very different perspective from that of France. For these fledgling democracies, being part of Europe seems almost entirely positive, not least because of the generous and well-deserved European structural funds accorded them for a couple of decades. Spain received about 1 per cent of its GNP from Europe for twenty years and many Spaniards felt it would have been churlish to vote No in their own, early referendum. The Spanish government wanted Spain to be the first to ratify the Constitution, told the Spaniards so and there was virtually no debate in the country – just a kind of rah-rah television campaign with sports stars and other celebrities extolling Europe and the Constitution.

We also need to acknowledge that the twelve newly acceded Member States are mostly run by elites who favour the economic model of the United States and have chosen NATO and the American shield for their security; meanwhile making the most of their comparative advantages in the European market – low wages, limited welfare systems and low taxes. We have given them precious few reasons or guarantees that would cause them to think differently. Plenty of Central Europeans feel rejected by France and the rest of "old Europe", as the Bush regime called it. Their governments will have no qualms in taking advantage of our weaknesses and, if they can, of our comparatively far greater wealth. It's up to us to show that the European project can be more than a free market and a cash register; that it can provide a decent, dignified and democratic – as well as a secure – existence for all.

Britain has always been a special case in Europe and it is no secret that the French often feel Charles de Gaulle got it right in trying to prevent Britain from joining the EU at all. I have heard murmurs, to which I have upon occasion added my own voice, that "opt-out" clauses should rightly be accompanied by "kick-out" clauses. Many Brits do not want to belong to Europe at all; whereas most of those who do seem to see Europe as a common market, period. My own views could hardly be further from these Tory-Tabloid-Tony Blair opinions and this will become clearer in the following chapters.

We, the French, also need to explain our "No" in order to contribute to the concept of a future European citizenship. How can anyone accept a Constitution – a document whose essence is to embody the expression of a people, as in "We the people" – if the people are nowhere to be found; if the people don't exist, or worse, don't even want to exist? How can we govern ourselves if we fail to develop a sense of specifically European citizenship and public opinion? If we fail to develop them, the market will irrevocably win because in a fragmented society only the market will matter; while society will be reduced to an undifferentiated mass of consumers. The technocrats and the elites will rejoice.

If we let the market win, there will still be battles to fight but the stakes in all of them will be depressingly similar. We shall be endlessly engaged in trying to stop yet another sector from falling prey to "free and unhindered competition" as the Constitution endlessly repeated; in clawing back a few basic workers' rights and preventing further deterioration of welfare; in clinging to public services for dear life and delaying the rise of inequalities...

I do not have a particularly theoretical approach to Europe, just a simple rule perhaps easier to follow for an American who chose the "Old Continent" decades ago. I just abide by my feelings, perhaps also a certain aesthetic. Aside from Paris where I live, I know instinctively when I'm in Europe. However different such cities may seem, I know I'm there in Madrid, Berlin, Ghent/Gand, Amsterdam, Edinburgh, Copenhagen, Stockholm, London or Lisbon; in Prague, Florence, Vienna or Dublin; in St Petersburg, Helsinki or Athens; even in Moscow or in Cluj (Romania). I feel less there in some neighbourhoods of Istanbul, but its university definitely feels European. I would undoubtedly feel just as much at home in many other European places I hope to visit one day.

My work has given me the great privilege and enormous luck of travelling widely in Europe, not as a tourist but as someone who is immediately plunged into local life and the company of the people who live there – an opportunity relatively few Europeans have so far enjoyed. Soon, however, more and more people will share the same kind of privileged existence I've had. Our young people are already spending terms or holidays in each other's countries; they will grow up speaking each other's languages, and despite the objections of the French who naturally think everyone should *parler français*, they will have English as a common tongue. Like me, they will feel at home anywhere in Europe and consequently they will feel European.

Later on, when they have joined the workforce, I hope they will also feel as concerned by a strike in Dresden or Naples as they would be by a conflict in their own home town. They won't need to define Europe because it will be part of them. Going to another country will be as easy as travelling to a neighbouring city in one's own country. For now, however, we have to get through a bad patch. The geopolitical cards are being reshuffled and we must be alert and as good at seizing opportunities as the opposition is. The French elites who told us Europe would be deaf, dumb, blind and paralysed if we voted No on the Constitution took less than a year and a half to concoct their equally dangerous replacement text, well hidden from public scrutiny.

As a French citizen and a committed European, I campaigned for the No with Attac and the "collectives" – between 900 and a thousand of these ad hoc groups sprung up all over France; every town and village seemed to have one. They included some political party members – often dissidents from their party's official stance – but also trade unionists, small farmers, students and teachers, environmentalists and other interested citizens. However, from February 2005, I set myself a complementary goal because it seemed important to write something short and to the point that could do the following:

- Show that Europe needs a radical change of direction, breaking in particular with the neo-liberal vision embodied in the Constitution;
- Explain – in case the Yes won – that all was not lost, that political-life-as-we-know-it would continue despite another victory for neo-liberalism and the failure of those struggling to break free from it;

- Suggest – if the No won as I hoped – how to move forward and consolidate the victory in the longer term and in many areas in order to renew politics not just in France but throughout Europe and, later on, worldwide.

Working towards a different Europe in a different world clearly did not stop with the victory of 29 May 2005; still less does it stop with this book. We are only at the beginning. I hope to make clear the underlying motives of the Constitution, analyse the behaviour of those who called for its ratification and propose foundations on which we could build an entirely different project.

Let me thank all those working toward the same objectives, in particular Sami Naïr with whom I had initially hoped to write this book. Although a joint project was finally not possible, he encouraged me throughout and was also kind enough to let me use parts of his initial contributions which he wrote in view of our collaboration. These excerpts are in Chapter 3.

I also want to thank the many members of the Attac Scientific Board (Conseil scientifique) who throughout the campaign produced analyses and arguments against the Treaty Establishing a Constitution for Europe, or TEC, the formal name and acronym I will sometimes use in the following pages. Occasionally I cite them but since we were all thinking along the same lines, I cannot promise to have disentangled the various strands and contributions. On the production side, I thank the Transnational Institute (my political home for over thirty years) for its support and Roger van Zwanenberg and Robert Webb of Pluto Books for their patience and forbearance faced with my delays. As someone said, "I love deadlines. I love the whooshing sound they make as they fly past": Roger and Robert weathered many gusts of this wind. As for the rest, the usual disclaimers apply and I am solely responsible for the content herein.

I'm not sure whether to thank the sheet of ice I slipped on one dark and wintry February night after a talk in Douai, but the resulting pelvic fracture did keep me housebound for several weeks which I used for research and writing instead of traipsing around the country campaigning. My ever-practical daughter Valerie took one look at me on crutches and said, "*Tu n'as qu'à écrire un livre*" – you'd better write a book. So that's what I did.

Timeline

Here is a reminder of the main stages of the construction of Europe.

1951: At the urging of Robert Schuman, the French Minister of Foreign Affairs, France and Germany merge the management of their coal and steel industries. They are soon joined by Benelux (Belgium, the Netherlands, Luxembourg) and Italy: the European Coal and Steel Community (ECSC) is born.

1957: The Treaty of Rome. In addition to the ECSC, two other organisations are established: the European Atomic Energy Community (Euratom) and the European Economic Community (EEC), which soon emerges as the most important among them. Together they are referred to as the "Common Market".

1958: Britain proposes that the "Common Market" be expanded into a vast transatlantic free trade area; the plan is vetoed by the French. The British then establish a similar organisation, the European Free Trade Association (EFTA).

1963: France vetoes Britain's EEC membership.

1967: The executives of the ECSC, the EEC and Euratom fuse to form the European Economic Community, which later becomes the EU. Its main institutions are:

- the European Commission
- the Council of Ministers
- the European Parliament
- the Court of Justice of the European Communities.

Additional institutions are the European Court of Auditors, the European Economic and Social Committee (made up of employees' representatives, employers, farmers, consumers, etc.) and the European Council (not to be confused with the Council of Ministers) composed of the President of the Commission, heads of state, and their respective Foreign Ministers.

1973: France lifts its veto: the UK, Ireland and Denmark join the EEC. Some continue to see the entry of Great Britain as "the fatal error". The next Member States to join are Greece (1981), Spain and Portugal (1986), and with the German reunification comes the de facto inclusion of former East Germany (1990).

1979: The Central Banks of the Member States sign an agreement launching the European Monetary System (EMS).

1986: The Single European Act amends the EEC treaties in order to reinforce Europe's capacity to establish a true common market. This is the first time social policies and aspirations are manifestly pushed aside. The social democrat Jacques Delors states that these will come "later".

1992: The Maastricht Treaty, ratified in 1993, brings the European Union into being and reinforces the EU's political role, particularly in the areas of foreign policy and common defence: the CSFP. The Member States decide to include the EFTA in the Common Market. Thus in 1995 Austria, Finland and Sweden join the EU. Norway chooses not to join.

1996: Crisis. France refuses to import British beef because of the "mad cow" epidemic. Britain threatens to "paralyse" the Union until the embargo is finally lifted in 1999.

1997: The Treaty of Amsterdam, following in the wake of the Maastricht Treaty, aims to create "an area of freedom, security and justice" and to "improve the relations between the Union and its citizens". Regrettably, it does not improve on social policy.

1998: Twelve countries set up the European Central Bank (ECB) to prepare for launching of the single currency, eventually named the Euro rather than the Ecu. The Euro, initially a unit of account among banks, becomes the official paper currency in the member countries in 2002. Unique among the world's central banks, the ECB is not subject to political control, and its only mandate is to maintain "price stability" (i.e. control inflation).

1999: Crisis. Allegations of corruption and mismanagement lead to the resignation of the Commission presided by Jacques Santer. A new Commission is nominated, headed by

Romano Prodi. The same year, the EU decides to incorporate a moribund defence alliance, the Western European Union (WEU), thus marking the first step towards the establishment of military and peace-keeping capabilities.

2000: The Treaty of Nice paves the way for EU enlargement. Against the Commission's will, joint decisions with Member States for commerce and trade in the areas of education, social services, healthcare and radio and TV broadcasting services are imposed. The Charter of Fundamental Rights is solemnly proclaimed.

2002: The decision taken by the Member States at the Laeken Summit in 2001 to prepare a constitutional treaty for Europe is implemented. A convention is appointed and mandated to prepare a Constitutional Treaty for Europe; it begins work under the presidency of Valéry Giscard d'Estaing.

2003: Individual accession treaties are signed with Cyprus, the Czech Republic, Estonia, Latvia, Lithuania, Malta, Poland, Slovakia and Slovenia. These countries officially join the EU on 1 May 2004, increasing its population by 20 percent and its area by 23 percent. The EU's first timid military efforts see contingents sent to the Congo, Macedonia and Bosnia.

2004: Following the June elections of the new European Parliament, the new Commission headed by José Manuel Durão Barroso takes office. Many consider it the most neo-liberal Commission in the history of the EU. The text of the Treaty for a European Constitution (TEC) is approved in Rome on 29 October. The 25 Member States begin the ratification process, some by parliamentary vote, others by referendum. The TEC must be ratified by all 25 Members to enter into force.

29 May 2005: French referendum on the Constitution: the "No" wins with 54.67 per cent of the vote and a 69.37 per cent turnout.

1 June 2005: Dutch referendum: the "No" wins with 61.6 per cent of the vote and a 64.8 per cent turnout.

Between June and October 2007, the Council expedites the presentation and approval of the Reform Treaty, virtually identical to the defunct Constitution, nearly all of whose "innovations" are incorporated. Eighteen Member States (including France) declare they will ratify the text via parliamentary vote; eight had not yet decided in November 2007; only Ireland must, by law, submit the Reform Treaty to a popular referendum.

A new chapter begins...

1
The War on Society

The 800-pound gorilla is sitting placidly in the middle of the room while everyone politely ignores it. This graphic metaphor perfectly describes a situation where people studiously avoid mentioning the issues central to a debate. The European gorilla, with his bottom squarely placed on the defunct-and-born-again Constitutional text, is called class war. Or if you find that expression too burdened with historical connotations, we can call it social war or a war against society; but some sort of war it certainly is. Neo-liberals from both the right and the so-called left are steadily undermining the European social system and pushing us backwards towards the frontiers of the nineteenth century.

The view I intend to defend is that European elites hope to lace people and their institutions into a neo-liberal straightjacket so tight it will take them decades to break free. The social-democrat leadership is following the same script and is so minimally social, or even democratic, that from now on I will call it social-liberal. When the campaign against the Constitution began in France, the elites did not realise how high the stakes were for them; they expected an effortless journey towards ratification of the TEC. The

French people, however, saw through their intentions and managed to make the elites' lives far more complicated. A majority saw what kind of future was on the cards and refused to be lulled into submission. In a matter of weeks, citizens by the thousands became Constitutional experts and developed detailed knowledge of European policies, never before a hot topic. The overwhelming success of the "No" shows that the Dracula strategy works: expose the creature to the light of day and it will shrivel and die. As the Reform Treaty demonstrates, the elites never abandoned their goal but for a time we were able to impede it.

I shall try to show that the European elites were and remain motivated by three complementary goals: **accumulate as much wealth as possible at the expense of working people, crush democracy and break the power of the State**. These are the components of a genuine social war. You think I exaggerate? Let's take a closer look at each of them in turn.

One needn't be a "vulgar Marxist" (or even a refined one) nor wait to hear the bullets whistling and the bombs exploding to recognise the signs of war. The great theorist of war Karl von Clausewitz wrote, "War is an act of violence whose goal is to force the adversary to do our will." Nor must violence mean bloodshed and broken bones – what is important is the will. The aggressor knows what he wants and his goals are opposite to those of his adversary. This is the ABC of war.

To reach those goals and force the adversary to accept them, one must first try to act through politics, for as Clausewitz also famously said, war is the "continuation of politics by other means". In other words, open warfare is evidence of political failure and visible, undeniable violence a last resort. Preferable by far is to ensure acceptance, internalisation and execution of "our will" without striking a blow. Decent people tend to disapprove of blatant force, at least in public, and the perpetrator should proceed subtly, in successive stages, moving forcefully only when the situation allows it, depending on the context and the adversary's will to resist. The aim should be to convince the adversary he is acting freely when in fact he is carrying out "our will".

The election of George W. Bush is an example of millions of people acting against their own interests; one could argue the same for the election of Nicolas Sarkozy in France. When millions of people, mostly poles apart from the elites, voted in favour of the Constitution, they too acted against their interests. Don't blame them – the elites devoted time, money and impressive skill to that end. Since they wanted their force to be invisible, let's now try to hold it up to the light.

Accumulating wealth

What does the international ruling class – and the European elite in particular – want? What are these people the *Financial Times* calls "masters of the universe" after; the ones who gather every year on the slopes of Davos? Could these well-dressed men and women, speaking perfect English and displaying impeccable manners actually be soldiers engaged in a social war? Might they possibly want to impose their will on an adversary who is – not to put too fine a point on it – us? Taken individually, certainly not. They haven't a bellicose bone in their bodies and are surely as kind to their children, their neighbours and their dogs as you and I. But as a group, as a class, the notion of social war looks definitely more plausible. Their goals have not changed over time. Adam Smith, revered by neo-liberals who have rarely read his work, was not afraid to name the gorilla. In *The Wealth of Nations* (1776), he points a stylistic finger at the "masters of mankind" and reveals the "vile maxim" that guides them: "All for ourselves and nothing for other people." The ruling elites have followed the vile maxim since the dawn of time, or at least since capitalism first appeared. Adam Smith put it like this:

> But what all the violence of the feudal institutions could never have effected, the silent and insensible operation of foreign commerce and manufactures gradually brought about. These gradually furnished the great proprietors with something for which they could exchange the whole surplus produce of their lands, and which they could consume themselves without sharing it either with tenants or retainers. **All for ourselves and nothing for other people seems, in every age of the world, to have been the vile maxim of the masters of mankind**. As soon, therefore, as they could find a method of consuming the whole value of their rents themselves, they had no disposition to share them with any other persons. For a pair of diamond buckles perhaps, or for something as frivolous and useless, they exchanged the maintenance, or what is the same thing, the price of the maintenance of a thousand men for a year[1] […]. (my emphasis)

Keep everything for yourself, then, and leave nothing for others. But what if the others refuse to go along? What if they believe that they too are entitled to something? In that case, you will have to use more forceful methods. What is Smith's "vile maxim" if not a declaration of war?

The same strategic goals have existed for centuries. The masters of mankind simply want to seize more power and wealth, at the expense of the vast multitudes below them, particularly those who believe themselves protected because their class is called "middle".

In the eighteenth century one could deprive a thousand men of their subsistence to buy diamond shoe buckles. Today the luxury goods would be different or – if you happen to be running a company listed on the stock exchange – you would deprive them in order to provide "shareholder value". It used to be that a company's success was measured by profit generated but this is now a dated or at least incomplete measurement. Profit remains important, but modern-day management gurus and rating agencies swear by "shareholder value".

This quasi-religious capitalist concept precedes, justifies and excuses everything. Even though one must make a profit, the real driving force is the share price that must relentlessly rise even though everyone knows that this "value" can melt away at the first signs of crisis. Mass redundancies and relocations in the name of competition and productivity contribute to the rise of share prices; they are thus by nature desirable. QED.

These worthy and deserving shareholders, who inspire all creation of value, have themselves evolved. We are no longer talking widows, orphans and small-scale savers whose banks have sold them mutual funds, nor provincial notables who were once content with ridiculous returns of a few per cent per annum. Such mini-capitalists are not now and never were in a position to complain. The shareholders one must satisfy now are those that economists call "institutional investors", and they are no laughing matter. They are large insurance companies, merchant banks, hedge funds, private equity funds, pension funds and, most recently, sovereign funds invested on behalf of governments from China to Dubai.

Frequently foreign-based, they control large proportions of supposedly national share capital. In France, for instance, the companies listed on the CAC 40 index are at least 40 per cent non-French owned and these powerful shareholders make demands consistent with their status. Worldwide, they soon figured out that they could claim annual returns of 5, then 10, then 15 per cent... the sky being the only limiting factor along with the amount of blood left in the company's veins. The press and the financial experts are always reminding us that "labour is too expensive". They're only kidding – what's really expensive for society is capital.

Transferring wealth toward the mega-owners of capital is nonetheless more complicated than it used to be. Although the victims rarely notice in time they are being fleeced, such habitual myopia is no reason for the masters to lower their guard. People may turn out to be tougher to fool than in Adam Smith's time; they can read and write (a big mistake, that) and may even have acquired some political consciousness. These upstarts think they have a birthright to certain advantages and have sometimes even organised themselves into unions. The masters must change tactics and nothing is more apt than simple procedures and complex texts.

Tax cuts for the wealthy are a case in point. No statistical evidence exists showing that higher economic growth correlates with lower taxes for the rich and for good reason – it doesn't. The rich have already satisfied nearly all their consumer wants, so the fiscal windfall will not notably change their patterns of consumption. They invest in shares instead, thus benefiting once more from "shareholder value". Tax cuts for the wealthy prove particularly costly and completely ineffective for encouraging economic growth but remain in place because the people they benefit are those who control such policies to begin with and because they conform to neo-liberal doctrine. The same inequalities can thus be perpetuated ad infinitum.

Another argument used is that lower corporate taxes make a country more attractive to foreign direct investment. This is the new mantra and comes in different fiscal flavours. The truth is that a country attracts investors because of the superiority of its infrastructure, the education and training level of its workforce and its quality of life; not because of slightly lower taxes.

The masters of mankind are not satisfied with this fiscal measure alone, and why should they be when one can go so much further down the same road? Consider the career of the "flat tax", peppered with paradox and small ironies.

In the Communist Party *Manifesto* of 1848, Marx and Engels advocated a progressive income tax with increasingly higher rates applied to each successive tranche. Decades later, the most advanced capitalist countries adopted this Marxist recommendation. Income taxes were never levied in the Communist countries because, by definition, everybody worked for the State. In 1998, Steve Forbes, a Republican candidate for the US presidency politically to the right of Bush (!), proposed that the progressive income tax (already much reduced since the Reagan years) be replaced by a flat tax with a single, low rate applied to individuals, consumption and companies. This is the one-size-fits-all T-shirt of the fiscal world, with no loopholes or exemptions (other than old-age pensions which remain untaxed). Despite Forbes' personal fortune (his father founded *Forbes Magazine*, publisher of the annual billionaires list), his bid for the presidency in general and his flat tax proposal in particular were seen as farcical.

The idea of a flat tax nonetheless continued to simmer in the think tanks of the American and British neo-liberal right such as the Heritage Foundation in Washington, the Hoover Institution at Stanford University or the Adam Smith Institute in London. Meanwhile, the USSR had collapsed and its former satellites were launched into independent orbits. Suddenly, young technocrats fresh out of American business schools were running these countries and one after the other, they introduced the now triumphant flat tax. The man responsible for Slovakia's finances tells visitors how he used to discuss the flat tax in seminars at Harvard but never thought he would live to see a life-size version of it in his own country, introduced by himself. The flat tax movement is gaining momentum.

Estonia pioneered it, soon followed by Lithuania and Latvia. Then came Russia, Ukraine, Serbia, Romania and Georgia. Slovakia attracted praise from competitiveness experts when it announced that the introduction of the flat tax led to 22 inward investment projects in 2003 and 47 in 2004, creating thousands of jobs. Poland joined the club in March 2005. Flat tax rates vary between 12–13 per cent (Russia, Ukraine, Georgia) and 18–19 per cent (Poland, Slovakia, Baltic States).

Hungary declared that it would not follow the fashion, but an opposition politician like Viktor Orban claims it is "inevitable" in view of their neighbours' situation. The Dutch Finance Minister Gerrit Zalm stated, "If old Europe cannot beat the flat taxers of new Europe, it may have to join them"; while the Spanish Prime Minister and German Chancellor ordered "serious feasibility studies". At that time, the German corporate tax was 38 per cent and 33.4 per cent in France; but these rates are at the upper end of the scale. The 15 Old European countries have already cut back: between 1996 and 2003, the average corporate tax rate fell from 39 to 31.7 per cent.

Neo-liberals appreciate the implicit message the flat tax proclaims: trust the market to deal with inequalities and social problems. Its champions point out that with such rates, it's not worth risking your reputation with tax evasion. Governments, they say, will also be better off because they will collect more. This happens to be true, at least for the time being: tax revenue in Slovakia and Russia has increased (although starting from a low level). Flat taxers also praise the simplicity of a system requiring only one-page tax-return forms and a pared-down bureaucracy. Anything resulting in "less State" is always welcome. They see the flat tax as "fair" because it does not "discriminate" between rich and poor and they reason that paying 180 euros if you earn 1,000 is the same as paying 18,000 if you earn 100,000. The flat tax is thus a shiny new weapon the masters can deploy in the social war. Bear in mind that the proposed Constitution allowed alignment (or "harmonisation") of tax rates only with the unanimous approval of all 25 (now 27) Member States. Since it is obvious that such unanimity will be forever unattainable, competition will ensure that the only direction taxes can go is down.

Whatever the fate of the flat tax in Europe, it will never be on the agenda of at least one country: the United States. There, building "tax shelters" is a thriving industry; the army of consultants, accountants, lawyers, and form-filling specialists it involves would fight tooth and claw any inclination to simplify a tax system which provides their bread, butter and caviar. Besides, wealthy Americans, both individuals and corporations, have a whole arsenal of dodges ensuring that they pay a minimum – which is exactly what the consultants, lawyers, etc. are for.

Whatever the 15 states of "old Europe" decide, they will inevitably be under increasing pressure to revise tax rates downward and corporations will use these moves to their advantage. Intra- and extra-European tax competition, aside from the hectic race to the bottom, will also provide an incentive for the new EU countries to use the only weapons they possess. In the language of neo-liberalism, the flat tax is a "comparative advantage". The impossibility of harmonising European taxes upwards under present European rules is one of the reasons I recommend much simpler "enhanced cooperation" (the EU term for coalitions of the willing prepared to come together around specific issues) combined with massive and accelerated development aid to Eastern and Southern countries (see in particular Chapter 3).

If you remain unconvinced that organised wealth accumulation at the top of society is underway, here is another subtle way to wage social war.

Economists call it "the allocation of added value". Calculating it is fiercely difficult even for specialists and fraught with methodological pitfalls, but all the applicable formulae lead to the conclusion that capital has steadily increased its share at the expense of labour. The OECD figures show "a collapse since the early 1980s in labour's share of added value throughout continental Europe and particularly in France".[2] In the mid 1970s, the share of added value allocated to labour reached its high point at 74 per cent but has since fallen to 60 per cent, meaning that capital's share has similarly climbed from 26 per cent in the mid 1970s to 40 per cent today. This deterioration of labour's share has also affected the US but this structural change has been more severe in Europe.

Other changes have accompanied this increase in capital's takeover of added value. As the authors of a Eurostat report note: "From 1996, expenditure on social protection compared to GDP continually declined through 2001; the ratio dropped by 2.1 points in [the Europe of the Fifteen]."[3]

Hatred of democracy

People have always tried to resist the accumulation of wealth and power in the hands of a few and have expressed their opposition through debate, the ballot box and in the streets. Such democratic expression is, however, less and less acceptable to the elite.

The golden age of neo-liberalism lasted approximately from 1980 to 1995 – the blessed Thatcher and Reagan years. The European Single Act was proclaimed in 1986 and neo-liberal momentum was accelerated by the establishment of the World Trade Organisation via the "Uruguay Round" (1986–94). Then came the secret negotiations of the Multilateral Agreement on Investment (MAI) hosted by the OECD between 1995 and 1998. Successive European treaties were meanwhile reinforcing the neo-liberal regime of the EU while the public remained, on the whole, blissfully unaware.

The first wake-up call came in France with the successful strikes of the winter of 1995–96, followed by a trans-national battle against the Multilateral Agreement on Investment which progressives were able to keep from coming into force. Their alliance defeated the MAI in an early surprise victory and forced the French government to withdraw. In December 1999, the huge demonstration in Seattle contributed to the collapse of the WTO Ministerial Meeting and since then, national and international anti-globalisation (at Attac we prefer the term "alter"-globalisation) movements have sprung up virtually everywhere. Since the onset of the new millennium, debates have been lively and social forums have thrived. Ever-stronger alliances are being built between unions, environmentalists, farmers, feminists, development and anti-poverty advocates and anti-globalisation movements.

Disaffection and distrust of neo-liberalism in Europe has had some impact on voting behaviour as well, including a disturbing increase in abstentions and in support for the extreme right which many working-class people see as defending their interests. Within the EU, millions feel excluded and protest whenever social "chainsaw massacres" and mass layoffs occur.

Retaliation by Smith's "masters of mankind" was to be expected. The history of social conflict offers few of those perfect moments when the elites can at a stroke undercut their adversaries. According to the logic of Clausewitz, that stroke should allow them to impose their will, secure their gains, perpetuate their advantages and make sure their power remains uncontested in the future. In 2005, that perfect moment had a name, the Treaty Establishing a Constitution for Europe, and a date, the referendum of 29 May. The elites also looked forward to savouring a delicious irony: the people, through a democratic vote, were going to sign democracy's death warrant.

The accumulation of wealth is doubtless the elite's primary objective; distrust of popular sovereignty and hatred of democracy are simply necessary if insufficient conditions to achieve it. Some of them have the frankness and decency to acknowledge it.

When a journalist asked Valéry Giscard d'Estaing if he regretted anything about the final draft of the Constitution, he declared:

> I was disappointed that very little attention was paid to people. Very little. There was tension about institutions, about the respective rights of the states and the Union, quite a debate. But not much for the people. But I perceive a demand from the people, so we should have gone to meet them, halfway or at least a third of the way, but we didn't…. You can't build a society purely on interests, you need a sense of belonging.[4]

True enough, but then what? If the 105-member Convention and its President paid so little attention to the people, it was doubtless because they had no place in the Constitution nor indeed in the Europe the text was intended to govern. The most basic right and duty of Europeans is to keep quiet and be content with whatever a benevolent bureaucracy and its leadership provide, i.e. very little.

The Founding Fathers of the United States, despite being mostly propertied and aristocratic gentlemen, began their preamble with the words: "We, the people... "* The first article of their Constitution declares that "all legislative powers herein granted shall be vested in a Congress of the United States, which shall consist of a Senate and House of Representatives", chosen by the people. Despite the manifold problems of American democracy, no one has ever tried to overturn this article.

The *Declaration of the Rights of Man and the Citizen* of 1789 was written during the first heady stirrings of the Revolution and embodies Enlightenment values. It proclaims that "The source of all sovereignty lies essentially in the Nation"; "The Law is the expression of the general will"; "Society has the right to demand accountability from all public officials for their administration."

The *Declaration* of 1793 (in fact the preamble to the new French Constitution) takes a stand against excessive accumulation of wealth and describes in detail progressive taxation and the "indispensable assistance that society should provide for less fortunate citizens", also described as "the debt owed by everyone who possesses more than he needs". The text affirms that "the people are sovereign; the government its handiwork"; furthermore, "the people can, whenever they please, change their government and revoke

---

* I can't resist quoting this great Preamble in its entirety: "We the people of the United States, in order to form a more perfect union, establish justice, insure domestic tranquillity, provide for the common defence, promote the general welfare, and secure the blessings of liberty to ourselves and our posterity, do ordain and establish this Constitution for the United States of America." That's it. The TEC's preamble is typically verbose.

their representatives". Human rights have no frontiers and imply solidarity within and between nations – "Men of all nations are brothers, and people of different nations should help each other according to their means just as should the citizens of the same State." The following statement from 1793 is also particularly relevant today: "He who oppresses a single nation thereby declares himself the enemy of all."

The French Constitutions of 1946 and 1958 also proclaim the principle of sovereignty defined as the "government of the people, by the people and for the people", echoing Abraham Lincoln here. Human rights are affirmed in its first articles, established in the name of the "French people". While it may be an understatement to note that these principles have not always been strictly observed, at least the sovereign people are always present and Enlightenment values are explicitly invoked as the foundations of society.

What, in Europe, remains of these virtuous, democratic and republican principles wrested from tyranny by our ancestors?

The TEC's preamble begins "His Majesty, the King of the Belgians" and goes on to list the royals and presidents who, a few paragraphs later, announce that they are "convinced that the peoples of Europe [...] are determined to transcend their former divisions and [...] forge a common destiny". All well and good, but these leaders and crowned heads never bothered to ask the peoples of Europe their opinion. The Europeans who drafted this Constitution were not elected but appointed and, unlike their eighteenth-century predecessors, the drafters did not even entrust the peoples' representatives in Parliament with the power to initiate legislation. In the text of the TEC, the Enlightenment gets short shrift, its values fade, the candles go out one by one and popular sovereignty becomes a dim memory.

The day after the referendum in France, Serge July's editorial leader in *Libération* expressed a similar hatred of democracy, reminiscent of Bertolt Brecht's remark about how governments should dissolve the people and elect a new one if the former misbehaves...*

Excerpts from July's piece entitled "A Masochistic Masterpiece":

> [...] a general disaster and a populist epidemic sweeping away everything in its path, European construction, the enlargement, the elites, regulation of liberalism, reformism, internationalism, even generosity [...], our country is in a sorry state. Unfortunately, it's in a worse state this morning.

Later I will discuss some provisions we managed to avoid – temporarily as it turns out – by voting against the Constitution. Before that, here are a few home truths concerning the so-called Charter of Fundamental Rights, which made up Part II of the TEC, solemnly proclaimed at the Nice Summit in 2000. In the Reform Treaty, they have stuck it in a Protocol. The parties on the right as well as the social-liberals made much of it but the rights it guarantees are often far less comprehensive than those declared in many national constitutions. Among the rights it does *not* guarantee are the right to work (the right "to work" and "to look for work" are quite different); the right

* "The people have lost confidence in the government. Perhaps the government should dissolve the people and elect another one." This was in East Germany in 1953.

to efficient public services accessible to all; gender equality and equal pay for equal work; unemployment benefits and a retirement pension; lifelong education, trans-national strikes; contraception and abortion; emergency medical treatment. Jurists may argue about whether all these have their place in a Constitution or should be codified in individual and separate laws, but since they are not to be found anywhere else in the European canon, the TEC was a missed opportunity to proclaim them.[5]

In any event, "This Charter does not [...] establish any new powers or tasks for the Union, nor does it change the powers and tasks defined in the other Parts of the Constitution" (II-111). So why go to the trouble of a Charter? As for those other "Parts", you can have democracy for minor issues but when it comes to economic choices, taxation, the currency, employment, employee rights, social policy and anything concerning war or peace, citizen interference is unwelcome.

European "institutions shall maintain an open, transparent and regular dialogue with representative associations of society" (I-47, 2). I personally experienced the meaning of this provision when many campaigners critical of the World Trade Organisation and Europe's pre-eminent role in it attended the "Civil Society Dialogues" initiated by Pascal Lamy, the then European Trade Commissioner. "Dialogue" meant explaining what the Commission intended to do. Any disagreement or criticism was seen as lack of understanding and duly met with a patient repetition of the Commission's position. "Civil society" mainly consisted of corporate and large agricultural interests and it was clear that Lamy, a member of the French Socialist Party since 1969, intended to use the European Union and the WTO as vehicles to promote global neo-liberalism. This was in any event his mandate from Member States.

For the past twenty years, the construction of Europe has been based solely on hugely complex texts, thereby shutting most people out of the debate. Non-elected bodies, European elites, corporate lobbies and social-liberals completing their conversion to Thatcherism have quietly altered the power structure to exclude the public even more. However, it is nowhere written that things must continue this way merely because that is how they began. We do not have to accept crumbs and defeatist mumblings that what we have is "better than nothing", or "Trust us and we'll deal with social issues later."

Let us look at a couple of recent instances of ignoring democracy. If ever the people of Europe made their voices heard, it was on 15 February 2003. From one end of Europe to the other, they shouted their opposition to the US-led Iraq war. A few governments, those of France, Germany and later Spain, heard them.

What could have happened if the TEC had been ratified? This is a speculative argument, but the proposed Constitution would have made enhanced cooperation between like-minded States easier in the areas of common security and defence policies (and extremely difficult in others). The text says "the Union's competence in matters of common foreign and security policy shall cover all areas of foreign policy [...] including the progressive framing of a common defence policy that might lead to a common defence" (I-16). Further, "the policy of the Union [...] shall respect the obligations of certain Member States, which see their common defence realised in the North Atlantic Treaty Organisation [...] and [shall] be compatible with the common security and defence policy established within that framework [that of NATO]" (I-41, 2). Finally: NATO "remains the foundation of their collective defence and the forum for its implementation" (I-41, 7). These provisions are retained and even strengthened in the Reform Treaty. These articles offer plenty of scope for supporting Bush's war and forcing the entire EU to follow. Nearly all the Member States belong to NATO.* The TEC also required European countries to increase their military capabilities and defence spending.

During the French campaign prior to the referendum, the social-liberals argued that the article providing for a citizen "initiative" was a victory for democracy. They took the risk of quoting the actual text, which did indeed grant that "not less than one million citizens [...] may take the initiative of inviting the Commission [...] to submit any appropriate proposal on matters where citizens consider that a legal act of the Union is required for the purpose of implementing the Constitution" (I-47, 4). In other words, if you thought the Constitution was not being applied, you and 999,999 others could politely ask the Commission to apply it, but you could not change anything you disliked in the Constitution itself, nor was the Commission required to act.

To conclude this short sampler of anti-democratic practices, let us note that normal democratic procedure includes the possibility of future Constitutional revisions and amendments. Here the TEC was streets behind the French *Declaration* of 1793 which proclaimed that "A

* Fortunately, military adventures could still be difficult to implement: "European decisions relating to the common security and defence policy, including those initiating a mission as referred to in this Article, shall be adopted by the Council acting unanimously" (I-41, 4).

people always has the right to review, reform and change its Constitution. One generation cannot subject future generations to its laws" (Article 28).

During the drafting of the European Constitution, some members of the Convention proposed that their own Convention could serve as a framework within which the text could later be modified. Others favoured a representative group of national and European parliamentarians. Both suggestions were still far too democratic for those who wanted a text engraved in stone. How, otherwise, can one interpret articles IV-443, 444 and 445 which call for double unanimity – first of the Council; then of every member State, either by parliamentary ratification or national referendum. With such impossibly tough requirements, the chances of modifying any established European policies would be virtually nil.

Furthermore, the entire text of Part III, Title III is specifically rendered permanent and unmodifiable. So what does Part III, Title III contain? Not much – only the internal market; the free movement of goods, services, capital and people; competition policy (including competition provisions applied to public services); taxation; economic and monetary policies; employment; social policy; economic, social, and territorial cohesion; agriculture and fisheries; the environment; consumer protection; research and development; technology; energy; freedoms, security and justice; border, asylum and immigration policies; police and judicial cooperation; public health; industry; culture; tourism; education; youth; sports; vocational training; civil protection and administrative cooperation.

Anything else could be changed except for defence and foreign policy, governed by similar restrictions.

Birth of a monster

How did we end up with a document as monstrous as the TEC? What strange process led to a text which, once its content was made public, could hardly be expected to trigger the enthusiasm of the French or anyone else who read it?

Some placed the blame on Valéry Giscard d'Estaing. In December 2001, he was appointed President of the Convention responsible for drafting the Constitution. The Convention's mandate encompassed about sixty topics, with the basic aim of creating a single treaty which would simplify and synthesise all the previous ones; organise the powers of the different branches in view of future enlargement to 25 or more members and reinforce the democratic legitimacy of European institutions.

Jacques Chirac, then French president, proposed his former political rival for the job, either because he forgave the many humiliations he had had to suffer as Giscard's Prime Minister or because he wanted him out of the country. When Giscard was President, cartoonists regularly drew him with crown and sceptre and he routinely instructed Chirac to walk three paces behind him. In 2003, the *Independent* published a portrait of Giscard: "Modesty and self-doubt have never been hallmarks of the former French president."[6] Others suspected his nomination as head of the Convention was a subtle way for Chirac to prevent him from interfering with his own re-election campaign for the presidency in 2002. Gerhard Schröder also weighed in for Giscard, probably recalling his cooperation with Helmut Schmidt in creating the European Monetary System, precursor of the euro. With this Franco-German blessing, all the other ducks fell into line. Giscard saw himself as a historical figure and had no qualms comparing himself to Thomas Jefferson.*

Once his position was secure, Giscard prepared for the historic task. According to *Newsweek*, he was about to set off on holiday and had three objectives:

> The erudite former French president, now 76, plans to go walking in the Loire Valley. He will perfect his studies of the Chinese language, and once again he will plough through the hundreds of pages of treaties and agreements that are the foundation for the European Union. "It takes a month just to read those texts," he says, "and Mandarin is sometimes easier to understand". But as chairman of the European Union's constitutional convention, he figures it's his job to pare those pyramids of paperwork down to some "30 or 35 pages in all" – something that's at once comprehensive and comprehensible, not to mention digestible, just like "the other great constitutions" of the world.[7]

Did he ultimately confuse the Constitution with Mandarin Chinese? The Convention did not exactly comply with VGE's hoped-for "30 or 35 pages". It produced, rather, a 232-page text (in the official French edition) with an extra 500 pages of appendices. It is "comprehensive" enough, especially if you want to cover economic policy in fine detail, but social policy is left vague or simply left out. Is

---

* VGE was apparently unaware that Jefferson, who was the author of the *Declaration of Independence*, was not part of the Constitutional Convention in Philadelphia in 1787. He was serving at the time in Paris as American ambassador.

it "comprehensible" and "digestible"? Possibly, for readers with advanced degrees, preferably in law.

For the duration of the Convention, serious disagreements arose between large and small, old and new, rich and poor Member States – but can these disagreements fully account for the anti-democratic monster born of the process? Might the MEDEF (the French employers' organisation) and UNICE (the European employers' organisation) have had something to do with it?* UNICE in its capacity as observer allied with extreme right Spanish MEPs and with the former Italian fascist Gianfranco Fini to insist that future laws and directives be adopted by the Council alone, without joint decision or even consultation with Parliament.

When the TEC was completed, UNICE declared itself well satisfied:

> The drafting of the article concerning the Commission corresponds to UNICE's demands for a strong Commission, keeping the exclusive right of legislative initiative [...]. UNICE is pleased that no proposals tending to introduce European-wide taxation have been retained [...]. UNICE is opposed to any extension of qualified majority voting to fiscal policy and is pleased to note that the unanimity rule will continue to apply in this area [...]. UNICE is satisfied that the objective of the European Central Bank

---

* UNICE, or Union of Industrial and Employers' Confederations of Europe, was founded in 1958. In 2004 its members included 38 central industrial and employers' federations from 32 countries. It is structured around five permanent committees, 60 workgroups and 45 employees, directed by a president and a secretary general. Since 1 July 2005 the president is Baron Ernest-Antoine Seillière, former president of the MEDEF.

will remain price stability and that its independence is guaranteed.

The European employers union's satisfaction also stems from the text's inclusion (in Article I-3 concerning the objectives of the Union) of the phrase "a highly competitive social market economy". From UNICE's viewpoint, this is a "considerable change because in the present [Nice] treaty, competitiveness is not mentioned". And it's even better that "competitiveness is reiterated in several articles of Part III". Pity the poor European Trade Union Confederation (ETUC) which thought it had won a great victory by getting the word "social" introduced just before "market economy". So did some German social-liberals. I think an impartial referee would give the goal to UNICE.[8]

The European Round Table of Industrialists (ERT) made up of the CEOs of Europe's 48 largest transnational corporations also played a role. Their contribution, later summed up in a brochure, was an argument for various neo-liberal policies. Corporate brass has consistently taken a keen interest in European construction and the Commission has always welcomed them warmly, as they did Baron Daniel Janssen, CEO of the Belgian chemical giant Solvay and member of the ERT. Janssen thus imagines Europe's future which he hopes will be based on a "double revolution"

reducing the power of the state and of the public sector generally through privatisation and deregulation and transferring many of the nation-states' powers to a more modern and internationally minded structure at European level.

Janssen expects the Commission to play a particularly important role in this "modern" structure because it is

> extremely open to the business community, so that when businessmen like myself face an issue that can only be solved politically, we have access to excellent Commissioners like Monti for competition, Lamy for trade, and Liikanen for e-commerce and industry.[9]

Thanks to these high-level contacts and to the 15,000 industrial and financial lobbyists based in Brussels, God's in his heaven; all's right with the European world; the Commissioners and Parliament will listen to business and tailor legislation to its needs. As the Commission itself said on its website about another neo-liberal text, "The GATS (General Agreement on Trade in Services) is not just something that exists between Governments. It is first and foremost an instrument for the benefit of business."

Above and beyond the easily discernible influence of big business, the Constitution also reflects the 105 people who drafted it, or more accurately commented on and amended the texts given them by Giscard and his immediate entourage. Convention members were not permitted to propose texts of their own. As we know, none of these Conventioneers was elected for this particular job although many were elected Euro- or national parliamentarians. This is a characteristic shared with only one other constitution I know of: the Constitution of the USSR, drafted by the unelected Politburo in 1936. The two documents also share the fine detail lavished on economic policy – albeit not the same kind of economics...

Giscard nonetheless set out with high hopes and some good ideas. "Should a small State be able to exercise veto power over all the others? With 25 or 27 Member States, decision-making would become impossible." Quite true. The cure for such paralysis was the introduction of qualified majority voting, often reduced to QMV. QMV, as he explained to a reporter for *Time Magazine*, "is what we will propose". He added that "We need to preserve the ultimate national right to dissent, not by blocking joint action, but by allowing governments not to participate."[10] In other words, countries that wanted to advance together should be allowed to do so through "enhanced cooperation" without being blocked by other Members.

The rabbit ultimately pulled out of the Convention's hat was of an altogether different breed. It set Constitutional rules which allowed *any* member, large or small, to "block joint action", notably in the areas of taxation, social policy and Constitutional amendment. Enhanced cooperation became immeasurably difficult due to various textual obstacles and traps.

Rumour had it that VGE had single-handedly drafted the parts of the Constitution touching on competences and attribution of powers to the various interested parties; legal experts then reviewed his texts. The proofreaders neglected to remove the comments of one of the latter; the mistake was only noticed when 162,000 copies of the French TEC (including mine) had already been printed. This nameless legal expert complained that

"Paragraph 1 contains a reference to the competences 'allocated to the Union in the Constitution' – another instance of contradictory and incoherent vocabulary used with regard to competences vocabulary...." (I-33)[11]

Like this specialist in contradiction and incoherency, some Convention members heartily disapproved of Giscard's drafts. One, requesting anonymity, confided that "[VGE] is capable of listening to twenty people, nineteen of whom have an opinion differing from his, and then declare: 'I am glad you all agree with me.'"[12]

To keep Tony Blair happy, Giscard promised to take an axe to the word "federal" each time it appeared. Downing Street noted that "He did everything we asked of him" and the *Daily Telegraph* rejoiced that Blair had "decaffeinated the text so it would not keep anyone from sleeping". Throughout the Constitutional process, Giscard and his Convention did whatever it took to satisfy the most anti-democratic forces in the European Union.

Break the power of the State

Any hope of imposing democracy at the level of the European Union is unrealistic (with or without a Constitution) within the present framework and in the absence of new political battles. For the moment, the only democracy within reach is that of the nation-state. The French and Dutch "No" votes proved that people can still trigger earthquakes through democratic means. European elites have taken this as a warning: to maintain control, they must quash popular power and emasculate the nation-states that allow its expression. The following personal/political anecdote can serve to illustrate the point.

In 2002, Attac confronted the General Agreement on Trade in Services, part of the World Trade Organisation treaty, and decided to fight back. The GATS treats education, health, culture, water services, public services and human activities in general as commodities and puts them all on a commercial footing. How could we best campaign? We knew it was futile to approach the WTO itself – it would reply that it was only acting as the secretariat for its 148 member states. You could sometimes disrupt the negotiations themselves, as in Seattle, but they invariably resumed a few days or weeks later. One could try to appeal to the European Trade Commissioner who negotiates on behalf of all the Member States, but with few illusions of being heard and no means of calling him to account.

GATS negotiations follow a "request–offer" procedure. First, the EU *requests* other, non-EU countries to open various service sectors to European firms. In the second phase, the EU *offers* to open some European service sectors to cross-border competition from non-European firms. In 2002, the European Commissioner for Trade, Pascal Lamy, made clear that none of the requests or offers would be made public, not even to the European Parliament, much less to ordinary citizens. His chief defence was that negotiations had to be intrinsically secret and "our [commercial] partners" refused that requests made to them by the EU become public. We – NGOs and associations – also had partners in non-EC countries and they definitely wanted to know what sectoral openings the EU was asking of their governments. Our concerns were not on the Commission's radar because from its perspective, it was none of our business anyway.

In the face of such opacity and contempt for democratic process, Attac teamed up with some MEPs in an attempt to force Lamy to appear at a "question time" in a parliamentary plenary session and we petitioned for the right to consult the request–offer lists. Pressure from MEPs (as well as leaked information) finally forced Commissioner Lamy to give in. It took months, but it finally became possible to view both the requests and offers.

Three years later, the new Commissioner, Peter Mandelson, casually announced that request–offer texts would henceforth be secret, using exactly the same arguments as his predecessor. The moral of this story is that trying to impose transparency, much less democracy, on the Commission is a labour of Sisyphus. We still had some democratic recourse nationally, so Attac-France launched a campaign for "GATS-free Zones". Eventually, thanks to a lot of speaking around the country, more than 800 local, departmental and regional councils declared themselves "GATS-free" and at least symbolically the zones covered more than four-fifths of the French population. The campaign was designed to educate the public and their elected representatives concerning the threat of GATS, a largely unknown quantity for both; but also to influence the French government because it was our only potential hope to change the EU Commissioner's mandate. As of this writing, the WTO negotiations, including the GATS, are on hold, but we probably had little to do with that. National action and lobbying is fraught with uncertainty, but it remains the only possible approach to democratising the EU.[13]

This concrete case illustrates the importance of maintaining the power of individual European nation-states to change the course of Europe if their citizens can force them to do so. Because this slim possibility still

We the Peoples of Europe

exists, European corporate elites want to reduce the space in which democratic governments can act since they could conceivably put the brakes on neo-liberal policies. No one expects European governments to act this way spontaneously and we understand that the Member States of Europe are themselves the constant targets of their own elites. Sometimes, however, a country does become the theatre of a successful social protest movement as we proved with the referenda of May/June 2005. It would be stupid to ignore this possibility and the French and the Dutch understood this.

So could Europe become a kind of super nation-state able to provide a genuinely democratic public space, concern itself with the common good and progressively increase the material, political, social and cultural well-being of all the peoples that make it up? Theoretically, yes. In practice, as matters now stand, no. For theory to become practice, many conditions would have to be satisfied. The European Parliament would need the power to initiate legislation and to oversee monetary and fiscal policies, marking an end to the total independence of the European Central Bank. Europe would need a much larger budget and the capacity to borrow (i.e. issue bonds) in order to undertake large-scale public works and invest in efficient, Europe-wide public services. The budget should supply massive aid to the new Member States and pay for democratic development in nearby Mediterranean countries and in Africa; we would make a huge research effort in basic science and renewable energy technologies, put in place a proactive social and employment policy – and much else besides. (We will return in greater detail to these matters in Chapter 3.)

But for now, you might as well say, "If we had some ham we could have some ham and eggs if we had some eggs." A social and democratic Europe presents exactly the same problem: we have neither the ham of democratic means to change nor the eggs of a coherent social policy. And Europe, as presently conceived, does everything in its power to protect Member States from the pressures put on them by their own citizens.

European elites talk about "competitiveness", stressing every syllable. They define it as the ability to sell goods at lower prices while using less labour (always remember that decent wages and social protection undercut competitiveness). The population should keep quiet because it doesn't understand economics and the market in its wisdom must be free to dictate the rules if we are to be successful. On the other hand, the elites are not much interested in shaping a successful Europe if "successful" means socially and economically just. They prefer the "Washington Consensus" and the neo-liberal recipes that have failed everywhere they have been applied – if failure means *not* achieving social or economic justice.

The French economist Jean-Paul Fitoussi brilliantly demonstrates that the ritualistic neo-liberal discourse on "competition"

> does not take into account the other determining factors of competitiveness, such as labour productivity, the concentration of high added-value activities in rich countries, the relatively high levels of capital stock, the degree of education, public investment in research and development, the importance of social cohesion.[14]

All these things require a State and Fitoussi shows that if a country is exposed to the shock of globalisation then in order to succeed, the population must be protected and the inequalities created by the market must be reduced through government action. The obsession with inflation and the restrictive monetary policies it requires should be abandoned in favour of full-employment policies. But rather than pursue such common-sense objectives, the EU makes sure Europeans are exposed to a double shock. First, each Member State has to compete with all the others *inside* Europe. The EU tacitly rewards the lowest bidder in European-wide "auctions" of wage, social and taxation policies. Second, European countries are together forced to face *global* competition – accompanied by reduced social protection and the elimination of national and trans-national solidarity.

When faced with globalisation, "less State intervention" is completely contrary to a winning strategy (supposing that this is the real objective). Again according to Fitoussi:

> new opportunities offered by opening up to trade and investment may allow countries to grow richer, but also exposes them to risk and harm. If these are not to cause irreversible damage to people, they must be protected more than before. A virtuous circle is created between international openness – that is to say globalisation – and economic security: openness increases the demand for security and satisfying this demand for security is an incentive to greater openness. Furthermore, the willingness of individuals to take risks depends on their degree of protection […].[15]

The true pro-Europeans vs. the elites

Despite the persistent efforts of the European elites, the European model undeniably exists. Despite its flaws and its variations from one country to another, it has solid foundations, it is codified in law, and establishes the rights and duties of citizens. It is inseparable from European identities, aspirations and ways of life.

The elites and their allies thought they could finally deal a fatal blow to all this and force Europeans into the neo-liberal prison with no alternative. The Constitution was their instrument of choice. Their war is waged not just against the least favoured Europeans – it targets young people and pensioners, salaried employees and the unemployed, native-born Europeans and immigrants. The traditional right and UNICE, with the social-liberals as accomplices, are all fighting on the same side. It's tragic, but it's the truth we must face.

The "No" struck a blow against this alliance but it must be the first in a series. We are not engaged in the classic war of capital versus labour that Marx and his many successors described – it's worse, because it has also enrolled much of the so-called opposition. Enough small and despicable people desperate to head even a minor ministry have sold out, dragging a lot of innocent voters with them.

The owners of capital in the traditional sense hardly need take the trouble to work directly and visibly for neo-liberalism – they have enough allies on the right and now on the "left". Although transnational capital employs the usual neo-liberal methods to accumulate wealth and resources, it is fairly confident that elections won't change anything fundamental. In the French case, whether Socialist, UMP

(Sarkozy's party), or anything in between, its interests are served, thanks very much. The French have often seen through the charade and regularly throw out those who forget their promises after a couple of weeks in office. They did it again on 29 May 2005 and they must try to do it in 2008 against the new Treaty. The right naturally defends neo-liberalism – what else? – whereas the Socialist leadership does not have the same excuse. I hope in this chapter to have shone a light on the gorilla, in fact the whole gorilla troupe. The gorilla at the centre of the European room is neo-liberal capitalism and its practitioners who betray the people, fear democracy and have nothing but contempt for the State and whatever is best in our traditions, our heritage, our culture and the European model itself.

The victory of the No gave progressive forces a temporary advantage.* The neo-liberal leadership thought the TEC would be accepted without a ripple and they were fooled into complacency. It won't happen again and the work has only begun, but the first step has been taken. In the rest of this book, I hope to make my own modest contribution to the renewal of this offensive – an offensive based on thought, example and action.

---

* An advantage that was needlessly and selfishly squandered in the lead-up to the 2007 presidential elections, but that is another story.

2

They Voted Yes, or Surviving on a Diet of Humble Pie

Valéry Giscard d'Estaing was pleased with his Constitution: "The text is easy to read, crystal clear and quite well phrased, which I can say all the more readily as I wrote it myself."[1] Indeed. Take Article III-192 for example:

> Without prejudice to Article III-344, to contribute to the preparation of the work of the Council referred to in Article III-159, Article III-179(2), (3), (4) and (6), Articles III-180, III-183 and III-184, Article III-185(6), Article III-186(2), Article III-187(3) and (4)...

It goes on like that for several lines but I will spare you the rest.

Did Article III-192 make you smile? It shouldn't: the European elite's capacity to increase its financial and monetary control over governments and ordinary citizens is not even vaguely amusing. The jargon paragraph establishes an "economic and financial committee" – part of the arsenal designed to help the Commission maintain budgetary discipline, guarantee capital absolutely unhindered movement and "promote [the] coordination of the policies of

Member States to the full extent needed for the functioning of the internal market". The text, however, has no intention of telling you so in plain language.

Complexity and disinformation

Mercifully, not all the articles of the TEC resemble III-192, but the text is nonetheless a jungle, a thorny thicket, an obstacle course. Those who govern us and those, like the social-liberals, who would like to govern us, use the well-honed tool of complexity. Texts which have an impact on our work, our rights and our lives, are increasingly indecipherable. The Constitution took impenetrability to new heights. We used to be able to make, or shout, simple statements like "US out of Vietnam", "CRS–SS"* or "Pinochet is a fascist" and – whether they agreed or not – people got the message. On 15 February 2003, millions took to the streets to deliver another simple message "No war in Iraq".

Today, politics relies on dense and obscure texts like the Multilateral Agreement on Investment (MAI), the General Agreement on Trade in Services (GATS) or the Bolkestein directive – the latter consisting of eighty pages of small print aiming to annihilate all social progress made in Europe since the Second World War. Citizen protests forced some changes but the directive is still dangerous.

The gold medal for longest, most boring and most incomprehensible political text still goes hands down to the Treaty Establishing a European Constitution (or did anyway until the Reform Treaty came along in its wake).

---

* The CRS, or Compagnies républicaines de sécurité are the most disliked of French cops. SS speaks for itself.

Its hundreds of pages seem designed to discourage even the bravest of voters including those with graduate degrees. In France, most people decided not to give up work, family or sleep in order to familiarise themselves thoroughly with the TEC.

Fortunately, many still did make that hard slog and these French supporters of the "No" published summaries, handed out innumerable flyers listing the most dangerous provisions and explained the text in thousands of meetings, allowing countless citizens to clear the wall of complexity and penetrate the TEC, despite the efforts of Giscard, the Convention and various governments. The campaign for the "No" was a sterling example of popular education and my colleagues from Attac, among others, can be proud of their achievement.

A good dose of courage was thus needed to conquer this Everest of a text, but also an eagle-eye to decode its terminology. In Euro-speak, the verbs are crucial and chosen with particular care when defining, for example, the objectives of the Union. In key areas like the market, the Union *guarantees* "the free movement of persons, services, goods and capital, and freedom of establishment". With regard to policies of Member States, which must be kept in line, the Union *coordinates*. The Union *offers* (thanks a lot!) its citizens "an internal market where competition is free and undistorted" – a pledge so important that it appears seven times in the text. The Union is also careful to declare that its laws and the TEC "shall have primacy over the law of the Member States" (needless to say, as this is the case for all treaties).

For sectors it considers of minor importance, like justice, social protection, sustainable development, social and economic cohesion, the Union *promotes* or *works for*. Sometimes it goes so far as to *aim for*, as in the cases of full employment and social progress.

In short, the drafters of the TEC forgot that the first and most important characteristic of a good Constitution is clarity. Perhaps they believed jargon would promote the victory of the "Yes", perhaps they couldn't avoid it, but whatever the reason, the complexity backfired.

The "Yes" camp on the right

Minister for research and former French astronaut, Claudie Haigneré bravely wrote that "pitting free competition against social protection is absurd [...], the Constitution gives more room to social protection than it has ever had before."[2] The text said otherwise, noting only that the Union and Member States *had in mind* "fundamental social rights [which] shall have as their objectives the promotion of employment, improved living and working conditions [...] so as to make possible proper social protection [...] and the combating of exclusion". A bit vague – having in mind doesn't necessarily mean you are going to fight for these objectives, but let's give them the benefit of the doubt.

The more relevant question is *how* they intend to provide "proper social protection" or combat exclusion. Can we count on the European budget, limited to 1.24 per cent of Member States' GNP; a budget which can be revised upwards only with the unanimous consent of all 27 governments? Even in the US, famously stingy in this respect, the federal budget allocated to social protection represents nearly 11 per cent of GDP.* Or perhaps the Europeans plan to do it through taxes, even though the European Parliament is deprived of any authority to levy them? They plan to use neither one nor the other. The TEC instead emphasises

> The need to maintain the competitiveness of the Union economy [...] such a development [towards social protection, against exclusion etc.] will ensue not only from the functioning of the internal market, which will favour the harmonisation of social systems but also [...] from the approximation of provisions laid down by law, regulation or administrative action of the Member States.

So once more, the message is: trust the market to bring forth justice, even though the Constitution does not tell us where this "development" (towards social protection etc.) is leading. The harmonisation ("approximation" in the English text) of social protection systems could very well take us to the sub-basement. Although the Constitution "encourage[s] cooperation between Member States", in social matters, such cooperation must occur while at the same time "excluding any harmonisation of the laws and regulations of the Member States". European law may – if the Commission deems it necessary – "establish minimum requirements for gradual implementation" concerning

---

* US GDP in 2006 was $13.392 trillion (US Bureau of Economic Analysis: www.bea.gov/national/xls/gdplev.xls). In the US budget document: Analytical Perspectives: Fiscal Year 2008", Table 25.9 ("Current Services Outlays by Function") gives a services total for 2006 of $1.320 trillion, comprising education, training, employment, social services, health, Medicare, income security, Social Security and Veterans benefits, or 9.9 per cent of 2006 GDP.

social questions, but only if it can simultaneously "avoid imposing administrative, financial and legal constraints". This is self-contradictory since any "requirement" implies either administrative or financial or legal constraints and probably all three. If you still haven't got the point, the text also calls for the Council to make unanimous decisions on social issues.[3]

In June 2004, well over half of eligible French citizens abstained from voting in the European parliamentary elections – only 43 per cent bothered to go to the polls. A year later, 70 per cent voted in the Constitutional referendum – the first time any European issue had captured the imagination of so many people. From the elite's perspective, abstention, whatever the stakes, can be a godsend. The ability of ordinary citizens to look after their own affairs *should* be reduced whenever possible – for the powerful, this is infinitely preferable. The more an issue appears distant, abstract and impersonal, the better. The public's ignorance is indeed bliss to neo- and social-liberals, whereas an informed citizen is dangerous. The Constitution seemed particularly well designed as a deeply off-putting and soporific document yet suddenly and unexpectedly, Europe and all its works became the centre of passionate attention.*

* In October 2007 as the token opposition to the Reform Treaty, I shared a platform in Brussels with, among others, the former President of Latvia, Dr Vaira Vikis-Freibergs. A perfect neo-liberal, she said that she knew from experience that politics and policy-making were full-time jobs and "people who make bread, or work in hospitals or... [various other professions followed]" should confidently leave these matters to the pros. So much for democracy. This is not the Soviet influence over Latvia speaking, as Ms Vikis-Freibergs lived most of her life in Canada before returning to Latvia as President in 1999.

The attendance at meetings was astonishing. I spoke in one village of 700 souls, children included, where 150 people turned up. In Toulouse, 5,000 people crammed into the Sports Palace with 5,000 more the security staff wouldn't allow in who listened outside. I was just off crutches and feared I might be knocked down in the crush. I witnessed normally peaceable souls practically coming to blows over the interpretation of this or that article; I saw loving couples shouting at each other at dinner. The best antidote to voting Yes was simply to read the text. That is precisely why its champions tried to avoid quoting it and preferred bland general statements. I debated with a pro-Yes Socialist MP simply by citing the actual text relating to each of his arguments and he kept trotting out the same blanket excuse: "This text is a compromise." Partisans of the Yes also tried to shame people: "If you vote No it means you're against Europe" (or the variant, "it means you're on the same side as the fascists"). Or they tried scare tactics: "If you refuse this compromise text, whatever you get later will be far worse." None of these arguments convinced the French.

The "Yes" camp on the "left"

The mainstream parties, including the Socialists, were all in favour of the Yes; everyone to the left of the Socialists was against it. The Socialists held an internal referendum early on, before people had time to familiarise themselves with the text and a majority of the membership duly endorsed the party's choice. Some Socialists like former Prime Minister Laurent Fabius broke ranks and called for a No vote. When time came for the referendum, according to exit polls, over half the people who identified themselves as members or sympathisers of the Socialist Party ended up voting No.

The far right, for quite different reasons was also in the No camp (about 17–18 per cent of the total according to most reliable estimates), many because they wanted to reject possible Turkish membership. Some people just wanted to use the occasion to give Jacques Chirac a slap in the face. The right behaved like the right always behaves and some French people who rather proudly identify themselves as "raleurs" or "grumblers", simply wanted to teach the government a good lesson.

I don't intend to discuss here the motives of these voters who acted predictably. The ones who present a real problem are the Socialists. I've shortened this section considerably in the English version so as not to submerge readers in needless detail concerning politicians they don't necessarily know or care about, but it is still worth examining the behaviour of these social-liberals and ask what political price they had to pay to stay in the Yes camp. In the title of this chapter, I refer to "humble pie" because they seemed prepared to swallow any humiliation without complaint. You be the judge.

A few leading Socialist lights

I argued earlier that the social war led by the neo-liberal elite and its allies has three major objectives: accumulating wealth and power, diminishing democracy and breaking the power of the State. I could have added others – rallying to NATO and American leadership, for example. In any war, the objectives are one thing, the strategy to attain them is another. Strategy is partly grounded in, and must be served by, rhetoric: you want to set the terms of the debate so that the adversary cannot stray outside your chosen vocabulary, you need to monopolise the conceptual framework and attack your adversary verbally to destabilise, disqualify and demoralise him until, ideally, he is reduced to silence.

In a social war you can't physically bludgeon your opponents so you must force them to fight on your turf, debate on your terms and react to your accusations ("No, I am not a liar; no, I do not hate my country or Europe"). It is better still if you can get them to accept even tacitly the labels you pin on them. Those who refuse your logic will automatically fall into the category of the ignorant, the pathetic, or the outdated. Plastered with insults, the adversary should have no choice but to internalise them, thus feeling not only intellectually inadequate but guilty.

The Socialist Euro-MPs

Eighteen French Socialists, acting or former Euro-MPs, were undoubtedly among the sharpest connoisseurs of the text and a couple of them were members of the Convention. While the text was being drafted, they formulated the following demands concerning public services and mandated their Convention members to get them included.[4]

The legal statute of public services must be consolidated and stabilised. Public services must be included in Constitutional Article I-3 concerning the objectives of the Union. A specific Title of the treaty concerning European policies must refine the European definition of public services, place the accomplishment of public service duties among the general objectives of the Union, distinguish paid public services from "services of general economic interest", ensure equal access through shared, proportional, financing and make State subsidies lawful whenever necessary. These new provisions must specifically exclude certain public services including health and education from the rules of competition and from international trade.[5]

These are praiseworthy, responsible, citizen-like objectives. The only problem is that not a single one of these demands was met or taken into account in any way anywhere in the final text. Other recommendations made by the same French Socialist group concerning economic, social, fiscal, agricultural or budgetary policies met a similar fate: they too were simply ignored. One would think these people would have wept or staged an open revolt watching *all* their demands being thrown out one after the other. Not at all. They supported the Yes to a man.*

In the Nice Treaty of 2000, public services – called "services of general economic interest" or SGEI in Euro-speak since "public services" are never mentioned – are listed among the "common values" of the Union. This was no longer the case in the Constitution, which merely speaks of services of general economic interest "to which all in the Union attribute value", without saying how much or what kind of value.

More ominous, public services are specifically subjected to competition: "Undertakings entrusted with the operation of services of general economic interest [...] shall be subject to the provisions of the Constitution, in particular to the rules on competition" (III-166, 2). SGEIs are never defined, and Member States are forbidden to pass or to keep on the books laws contrary to the Constitution, specifically to its

---

* But not to a woman: Socialist MEP Pervenche Beres, a supporter of Laurent Fabius, came out in favour of the No.

Articles III-161 to 169. These articles are precisely the ones that govern competition.

Who, then, is to decide whether a State has passed or kept a measure contrary to the rules of competition? The Commission, of course, who else? It "shall ensure the application of this Article and shall [...] adopt appropriate European regulations or decisions". Just as you would entrust your hens to the fox, or your lambs to the wolf, the SGEIs are entrusted to the European executive, which over the years has seized every opportunity to privatise or dismantle them.

Sorry as I am once more to inflict Giscard's prose upon the reader, this ordeal is necessary. To make things clear from the start, the text reads, "any aid granted by a Member State or through State resources in any form whatsoever which distorts or threatens to distort competition by favouring certain undertakings... shall... be incompatible with the internal market".

Public services are by definition subsidised and not sold to the public at their "true" (meaning purely economic) cost precisely because their value to society lies elsewhere (e.g. efficient public transport or communications). Therefore subsidies have to "distort competition" – that is exactly what they are meant to do. Having thus delivered the *coup de grâce* to subsidies, the Constitution drives another nail into the coffin of public services, announcing that the top-cop Commission "in cooperation with Member States, shall keep under constant review all systems of aid existing in those States [...]. If... the Commission finds that aid granted by a Member State or through State resources is not compatible with the internal market... it shall adopt a

European decision requiring the Member State concerned to abolish or alter such aid" (III-168).

European socialists and the French Socialist Party defended the Constitution on the grounds that it provides a "true legal basis" for public services (or rather for SGEIs, not the same thing); they simply omitted to note that this true legal basis is one that encourages and is intended to preside over their demolition and disappearance.

Are you still a bit confused about European provisions regarding SGEIs? Not to worry. You can check out the diagram below to see how simple and easy to understand these provisions really are.

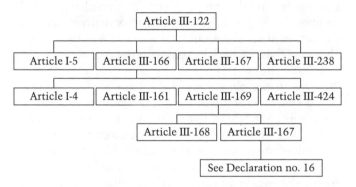

The European Trade Union Confederation

As the drafting of the Constitution proceeded, the European Trade Union Confederation (ETUC) also voiced concerns about public services and duly submitted a list of demands to the Convention, listed here in summary:

The term "social market economy", as well as "full employment" and "economically and socially sustainable development" must figure among the objectives of the Union. Employment must be integrated into the principal orientations of economic policy; matters of taxation must be decided by qualified majority voting, not unanimity; the mandate of the European Central Bank cannot be limited to price stability but should include growth, investment and employment.

As with the Socialist demands, there is nothing here that decent, well-intentioned people would not applaud. And once more, the only term retained after a lengthy battle is the ambiguous "social market economy". However, to satisfy the employers' union UNICE, it is preceded by the words "highly competitive". The resulting "highly competitive social market economy" actually cancels out the notion of a social economy.* As we saw in the previous chapter, UNICE was delighted with the result.

ETUC thought itself lucky that full employment "figures in the objectives of the Union", but the trade union confederation was really indulging in a bit of feel-good point-stretching here. The full text refers only to "a highly competitive social market economy, aiming at full employment and social progress". One can "aim at" anything for years without necessarily reaching the target. As for the means to reach it, the Confederation did not manage to expand the Central Bank's mandate to include

---

* I learned much later that European Protestant churches, particularly in Germany, went through similar debates on the same terms. While the more conservative elements were satisfied by the inclusion of "social market economy", the more progressive ones argued, correctly in my view, that the phrase meant nothing, just as UNICE had itself foretold. "Social" is everywhere trumped by "market" and by "free and undistorted competition".

growth and employment. Usually displaying quasi-saintly forbearance, the ETUC did show signs of irritation in June 2004, reporting "genuine frustration and increasing disappointment in trade-union circles" regarding the Constitution. It called for a "Europe working for people, not companies".

Despite this frustration and the demonstrable lack of interest in their requests, the ETUC ultimately came out for the Yes. A sizeable part of its budget comes from the EU: this may or may not influence its policy decisions. The Confederation furthermore sits alongside UNICE as a "social partner" of the EU and this status lends prestige. Despite the formal decision, a great many rank-and-file trade union members and even some ETUC member-unions refused to approve the TEC. One high level dissident was a former president of the Confederation, the Belgian Georges Debunne, who also campaigned for the "No".

The French Socialist Party brass

About a year after their 18 MEPS had submitted their (unmet) demands to the Convention, the French Socialist Party officially submitted its own.[6] Mostly these were a kind of ritualistic rehash, like the ones concerning public services, taxes on capital movements, changes to the Central Bank's mandate, qualified majority voting rather than unanimity on social and fiscal measures, enhanced cooperation and many more. There were, however, a couple of novelties. One concerned secularism.

It is sometimes difficult to convey to outsiders how important the notion of "laicité" is to the French, imperfectly translated as "secularism". The Republic and the Catholic

Church fought for primacy during the entire century that followed the French Revolution, itself a crucial anti-clerical milestone. Finally, in 1905, in a stunning victory for the Socialists of that era against the clericalists, they got a ground-breaking Church–State separation law to which not only Socialists but all French "republicans" remain deeply attached. The "headscarf law" was resented and criticised in some left circles abroad, particularly in Britain – but in France, people do not want to go down the "communitarist" road and start recognising special rules for this group or that. You can do whatever you like in private, you can wear a headscarf in the street, in the supermarket or in the metro, but when you are on the terrain of the Republic, such as public schools, there is one law for all and it excludes (and has always excluded) large and visible religious symbols. A cross, a star of David or a crescent on a chain around your neck is OK anywhere. So it was understandable that the French SP did not take kindly to references in the TEC to the European religious heritage and especially not to Article I-52 which for the first time in European history put the relationship between the EU and religious entities on a compulsory footing. "Recognising their identity and their specific contribution, the Union shall maintain an open, transparent and regular dialogue with these churches...."

This was bad enough, but many Socialists found Article II-70 positively alarming, promising as it did that "everyone has the right to freedom of thought, conscience and religion". So far so good. But then the text says that this right includes "...freedom, either alone or in community with others and in public or in private, to manifest religion or belief, in worship, teaching, practice and observance".

Individually or collectively, in public, through practice and observance? Couldn't that overturn the "headscarf law" and any similar laws? At least one French Muslim organisation thought so and came out for the Yes, promising to test the law against Article II-70 in the European Court of Justice.

But once again, no changes were made to the text and the SP remained officially on board with its First Secretary François Hollande positively oozing approval:

> "In this treaty there are only steps forward; not the slightest step backwards. [There is] not the slightest risk of losing our social model, not the least risk, present or future.... If I had identified the smallest backward step, the tiniest risk, the slightest threat, today as First Secretary, I would not call for a Yes vote."[7]

One feels Hollande didn't look very hard. Aside from the several dangers already cited, we could add that Article III-156 wiped out any possibility of taxing cross-border capital movements within Europe or even between European and foreign countries – a prime objective of Attac which the Socialists had initially refused but finally asked for. Further, although the Socialists had called for "a Europe capable of acting as a counterweight in the world to United States unilateralism", they seemed to have no objections to primacy of NATO in the area of common defence and security.

Maybe my definition of "American unilateralism" is different from that of the Socialists, but if Europe really intended to "act as a counterweight" to American power, would it not need to possess its own, independent defence capabilities? In any case, French Socialists did not seem disturbed that the TEC makes that impossible.

The rule is that "Commitments and cooperation in this area [i.e. the area of defence and security] shall be consistent with commitments under the North Atlantic Treaty Organisation, which, for those States which are members of it, remains the foundation of their collective defence and the forum for its implementation." Until further notice, NATO is a military organisation led by the United States army, with George W. Bush acting for the moment as commander in chief. Why should a unilateralist United States bother to take European interests into account? Europe is no longer a strategic priority for America and the US is gradually dismantling its bases there in favour of a stronger presence further to the East. The TEC requirement (in Article I-41, 3) that "Member States shall undertake progressively to improve their military capabilities" is not exactly reassuring either. We shall discuss military and geopolitical matters in more depth further along.

I've already noted Downing Street's satisfaction with the "decaf treaty" guaranteed not to keep Britain awake at night. An English specialist tells how, during the negotiation of the Nice Treaty (signed in 2000), the British worked in close cooperation with the US and with the support of other European NATO members. The joint purpose of their manoeuvre was to prevent the EU from becoming the "European pillar of the Atlantic alliance" which should be instead – still according to the Brits – "a common structure in the hands of a common authority". Obviously such a "common authority" would be heavily weighted towards the United States. The TEC consolidates the victory of NATO and US-dominated Atlanticism, so it is harder still to understand Socialist enthusiasm for this treaty if they were genuinely opposed to them.[8]

Another prominent – and snubbed – Socialist

In 2007, the French Socialist Dominique Strauss-Kahn, nominated by President Sarkozy, was confirmed as the new Director General of the International Monetary Fund. It is not his first international mission. At the request of Romano Prodi, "DSK" (as the French press usually calls him) chaired a "Roundtable" of eminent Europeans called upon to recommend ways Europe could move forward politically. In 2004, they submitted their final report containing "50 Proposals for the Europe of Tomorrow" that have Strauss-Kahn's fingerprints all over them.[9]

Take my word for it – it's a great report and one can applaud nearly all the proposals. For example, few would quarrel with giving absolute priority to research with a meaningful budget of 0.25 per cent of European GDP, compared to the miserable 0.04 per cent we have now, and making massive investments in higher education so that half the European population will eventually hold a university degree. Starting immediately, all students would be required to spend at least a year studying in another EU country; language training and life-long learning would be stressed, along with much higher financial allocations to education and culture.

Europe needs exactly such a programme because it is clearly lagging behind in research and higher education. Some 400,000 European scientists, often the most highly qualified (and trained in *our* schools), are now working in the United States because the labs there are Paradise Regained whereas those in Europe are often Paradise Lost. They can also make a lot more money.

According to a European Commission study, three-quarters of the European scientists who did their PhD or post-doc work in the United States between 1991 and 2000 have no intention of returning to Europe. The European trade deficit in "high-technology" products was "only" €9 billion in 1995; it skyrocketed more than fivefold in five years, to €48 billion in 2000.[10]

This is not the way to become the "knowledge-based economy", the EU Council glibly called for in Lisbon in 2000 (and has repeatedly called for since).

DSK's report recommends concentrating public social spending on those who need it most, beginning with early childhood (along the lines of the highly successful Danish model) and in underprivileged urban areas in order to promote genuine equality of opportunity. All European citizens would enjoy "career development security". Social rights like pensions, health insurance, unemployment compensation and so on would be fully transferable from one European country to another. Special assistance programmes would be created to encourage intra-European job mobility, help victims of company relocations and rebuild after natural disasters. A European minimum wage would be introduced, calculated for each country using a common formula. The growing numbers of European senior citizens would benefit from a programme modelled on the World Health Organisation's "Active Ageing" policy framework.

To make all this easier, tax and social competition would be eliminated because they are "incompatible with the European model" and 66 "disloyal" European tax-havens identified by the Commission would be outlawed. So would several tax havens where rich European individuals and corporations can park their money. Although the report does not go so far as to call the statutes of the European Central Bank into question – among the eminent European members of the Roundtable was the arch-orthodox Hans Tietmeyer, former governor of the Bundesbank – it does advocate sharing responsibility for monetary policy with the Euro-group which should have official political as opposed to ad hoc standing. Euro-currency countries would become joint decision-makers with the Central Bank and speak with a single voice in international institutions like the IMF and the G-8.

The report also calls for revamped industrial and employment policies to promote major common industrial projects like Airbus and Ariane that could compete globally. This would mean revamping European competition policy from scratch. Policy should encourage more cooperation among Europeans and integrate European infrastructure, beginning with railways. Infrastructure would get 0.25 per cent of European GDP rather than the puny 0.01 per cent currently allocated. Start-ups and innovative SMEs would benefit from special funds and credit arrangements.

DSK sought also to put an end to a two-speed Europe with pace-setters and laggards. This would mean a significant increase in the Structural Funds budget set at 0.6 per cent of GDP, so as to repeat the successes of the PIGS (Portugal, Ireland, Greece and Spain) in the newly acceded countries. The environment would also get special attention and here Europe should set an example for the world. No public contracts would be signed without strict environmental specifications. Agriculture should become less intensive and more ecologically friendly.

To give European citizens a sense of belonging, the President of the Commission and his/her commissioners would be elected and a given proportion of MEPs would be chosen from common European lists. Official Overseas Development Aid would finally attain the 0.7 per cent of GNP set by the United Nations decades ago and Europe would practise enhanced cooperation with countries around the Mediterranean. It would also initiate two World Funds, one for health, the other for water. European defence would focus on multilateralism and "soft power" so that Europe could become a global force for justice and peace.

Is all this too good to be true, a total utopia? Not according to the eminent persons and experts present at the Strauss-Kahn Roundtable. Such an ambitious programme would, however, require a serious financial overhaul and funding would depend – says the report submitted in 2004 – on the future European Constitution. Strauss-Kahn denounces the "dwarf budget" that has kept European spending at a mere 1 per cent of GDP and fixes the budgetary ceiling at 1.24 per cent. Necessary changes would require that Europe

- take more decisions through qualified majority voting, especially for social, fiscal and foreign policy matters;
- remove the ceiling on the budget and at least double it;
- give the European Parliament the power to levy taxes, beginning with a 1 per cent Europe-wide corporate tax;
- revoke the Central Bank's mandate as sole arbiter of monetary policy and give the now informal Euro-

group official status with the goal of creating a kind of collegial and political Ministry of Finance;
• abolish tax havens.

The priority of priorities for DSK and the Roundtable members is, however, the leeway to revise the Constitution. Member governments must give the next European Parliament a mandate to undertake a new phase of the Constitutional process because the present text needs basic changes. As things stand, "the amendment-revision process is particularly ill-suited and carries the risk that the treaty will be 'frozen' in a Union of 25 members". Strauss-Kahn hammers the point home once more in his report's conclusion:

Most important of all, the content, particularly that dealing with Union policies, must not be set in stone: if there were but a single subject the Heads of State and Government should continue to discuss, it is the future arrangements for revising the Constitution.[11]

Nobody paid the slightest attention. The heads of state and government were content with a text ensuring exactly the "freeze" DSK feared. Revision would be possible only with double unanimity (by the Council and by individual ratification in all Member States, via parliamentary vote or referendum). Neo-liberalism emerged once more triumphant, whereas Strauss-Kahn's report repeatedly stressed that if the TEC was not changed, particularly the revision process, we could kiss the European model good-bye as it could not long survive.

What would you do if you were in his position? Make a huge fuss and come out clearly for the No, explaining why? Refuse to take part in the sham of recommending the Yes and go abroad for six months? What he in fact did, like virtually all the top French Socialists, was to campaign fervently for the Yes. The first possible explanation is that he didn't believe a word of his own report and didn't care that the Constitution nullified or rejected all its proposals. In this case, he was quite prepared to accept, based on his own analysis, a stunted Europe with no future.

The second explanation is that, although he believed that the report's recommendations were vital for Europe's future, he was still ready to eat humble pie and not fight for them, judging that a Yes vote to the text would provide himself, DSK, with more scope to play a powerful future role. In this case, he was rewarded, a safe and sage choice for the new rightwing president to send to the IMF. I am unable to identify a third possibility unless it is "party loyalty" of a quasi-Stalinist variety. My own view is that he hoped to be the Socialist presidential candidate in 2007 but lost out to Ségolène Royal. He couldn't foresee that he would be picked for the IMF, but such an honour would surely not have been bestowed on, say, Laurent Fabius – just as competent as DSK but who favoured the No.

At every stage of the European project, at least since the Single Act of 1986, the same people have used the same arguments: Europe is the future, Europe is modern and dynamic, but above all, Europe is a market. We're sorry, we can't yet offer you much in the way of social policy, maybe your quality of life has gone downhill in the past 15 years or so; we regret this just as much as you do, but one day social Europe will happen, so trust us, don't worry, we're working on it. But first, the highly competitive market must be really, truly, perfectly in place. The four freedoms – movement of goods, services, capital and people – must proceed without let or hindrance, while never forgetting the fifth freedom, that of commercial establishment. When all this is granite-hard, we can think about the rest.

The French Socialist Party's Yes campaign chose the slogan "And Now, Social Europe". What do you mean, Now? Who do you think you're kidding? The leadership (because I am not blaming the rank and file) cooked up what the French, who like culinary metaphors, call "lark pate" or *pâté d'alouette*, composed of one (economic, competitive market) horse and one (social) lark.

One has to ask at what point one has to stand up and say enough is enough or totally lose one's honour. Perhaps the SP wanted to follow the lead of the Spanish (Socialist) Minister for Justice Lopez Aguilar who declared "You don't need to read the European constitution to know that it is good."[12]

In any event, they did not stand up and they did not say enough is enough. Social liberalism is here to stay. The Reform Treaty is OK with them too, and they won't even call for a referendum. Previously left-of-centre parties have taken the same route all over the world – including British Labour with the Third Way or the Democrats in the United States who also seem to thrive on concessions to the right.

Peter Mandelson, the European Trade Commissioner, perhaps put this attitude most succinctly. After Socialist defeats in France, Italy and Denmark, he had a flash of inspiration and announced his conversion to the assembled Blairites:

"No serious challenge on the Left exists to Third Way thinking anywhere in the world.... and in the urgent need to remove rigidities and incorporate flexibility in capital, product and labour markets, we are all Thatcherites now."[13]

So accept capitalism and the market forever, both theoretically and practically. Capitalist globalisation is neither a problem to be solved, nor a force one can criticise, much less overthrow. In the words of Margaret Thatcher, "There is no alternative."

Following the publication of Mandelson's comment in *The Times*, a Tory slyly remarked, "It is astonishing that it took Mr. Mandelson so long to reach the same conclusions we reached long ago."

What does being a "Thatcherite" imply? People in Great Britain know the answer. It means believing in and working for market freedom, monetarism, privatisation and tax cuts for the more fortunate, resulting in greater inequalities. It means standing tall against unions and demonising the Welfare State. It means negating the European model (which I personally see as one of the more important achievements in human history). As Mrs Thatcher herself put it, "There is no such thing as society."

Progressives believe, rather, that social cohesion is important and life in a democratic society depends on setting limits to economic freedom. The "sovereign" alone can set these limits. Enlightenment philosophers believe that if sovereignty resides in the people, the State issuing from this sovereignty will arbitrate between different interests, ideally to impose the common good, practically in function of the balance of forces at a given time.

If on the other hand the sovereign is the market, it will organise society in such a way that economic freedom will be foremost. Society will be atomised and citizens will become mere individuals, or "consumers". Little by little, in the absence of social cohesion, society and life itself will become unbearable.

Peter Mandelson and his social-liberal counterparts have chosen the slippery slope. I prefer the nineteenth-century French reformer and Dominican priest Henri Lacordaire who recognised that economic freedom by itself is no freedom at all: "Between the strong and the weak, between the rich and the poor, between the master and the slave, it is freedom that oppresses and the law that frees."

3
The Common Good:
Towards an Alternative Europe

A month and a half before the referendum, the polls were heading straight downhill for the Yes camp. The commercial, pro-government TV channel TF1 hastily pulled together a cross-section of "representative young people" to question Jacques Chirac, bringing out their biggest gun in hopes of shooting down the opposition. The young people were concerned about lousy jobs, casual jobs or no jobs; affordable housing, the lamentable state of the universities and other unimportant, mundane matters. The President explained to them that if they voted No, France would become the black sheep of Europe. They looked unconvinced; so was the TV audience.

Better a black sheep than simply a sheep – at Attac we had black sheep badges made up and wore them with pride. A more suitable metaphor, assuming we should stick to the animal kingdom, would have been the ugly duckling that turned out to be a swan. Most progressive Europeans and democrats did not see the French as outcasts but were grateful to them for stopping a detrimental process.

The French summoned the courage to confront the political, financial and media elites who demanded agreement and a docile "Yes". Hell hath no fury like an elite scorned and one could measure the scope of the victory by their rage. They understood they were losing influence. We have already quoted the angry outburst of Serge July, editor of *Libération*, and his contempt for the electorate; speaking of a "general disaster", a "populist epidemic", a "masochistic masterpiece". My favourite quote, however, comes from the Vice President of the Commission, the Commissioner for business and industry Günter Verheugen who exhorted his colleagues after the French and Dutch votes: "We must not give in to blackmail." So much for universal suffrage. Verheugen has that neo-liberal spirit and may yet supply us with as many choice aphorisms as ex-Commissioner Frits Bolkestein once did.

As we develop future strategy, we must foresee the probable responses from the elites because they will inevitably try to stifle the voice of popular dissent. Their challenge is to break the momentum of protest and get everything back under control. We should avoid handing ammunition to the frustrated neo- and social-liberals. Non-French European elites in particular will appeal to the common stereotypical image of "arrogance" that allegedly inclines France and the French against cooperation with others. Serge July used the cliché himself in the same editorial: "France exists because it can singlehandedly unhinge Europe. On your knees, Europe, bow to our 'No'." Fortunately for those of us in the French No camp, the Dutch, reputed for their moderation and modesty, also voted Nee.

The disappointed, frustrated and discredited opposition also tried to convince the rest of Europe that the French No was motivated by xenophobia and prejudice against immigrants, either Central European or from farther afield.

During and after the referendum, the French and European media got full mileage from this myth, often trotting out the valiant "Polish plumber" we were supposed to fear because he was out to steal our jobs. The ubiquitous plumber was actually the brainchild of Frits Bolkestein and he – the plumber, not the Commissioner – seems to have been busy unblocking drains all over Europe, thereby providing a convenient, if phony excuse for bashing the No forces.

During the campaign, the right constantly brandished the spectre of chaos which, if the No were to triumph, would surely ensue the following morning. The Constitution, they assured us, was all or nothing: there was no Plan B to fall back on, and if the No passed we would be taking an historic risk and responsibility. Luckily, most people ignored the warnings and in fact, between 29 May 2005 (date of the referendum) and the end of June, the euro–dollar exchange rate dropped from 1.23310 to 1.20920 – not exactly the crash of the century and rather good news for European exports even though it slightly raised the cost of oil. No chaos, no drama, no nothing – on 30 May we simply resumed living under the Nice Treaty as we had done since the year 2000.

Now, two years after the referendum, the political task of creating another Europe is the same but the balance of power, which the No momentarily shifted in favour of the progressive camp, has been utterly transformed. With characteristic skill, the French left has snatched defeat from the jaws of victory and is much weaker than it was in May 2005. The elites didn't need to do anything – the "left of the left" and the French Socialist Party did their work for them. So far, President Sarkozy has manoeuvred brilliantly to keep them powerless and reeling. It is hard to know how we can go about altering the Europe that now faces us but we must nonetheless try. So I intend to write as if we – not just the French but all the peoples of Europe – could continue to push for an alternative European Union, because if we don't, we know the wrong people and the wrong policies will win.

This chapter will thus not concentrate on post-mortems, however necessary self-critical examination may be, but rather on the need to forge a genuine, European-wide public opinion while recognising this will be a long term task. All the progressive forces throughout Europe – political parties, trade unions, citizens' associations, solidarity organisations and social movements – must now help promote a true European debate in a very short time. We must simultaneously explain what was (and remains) wrong with the Europe the elites are determined to impose upon us and begin to build the foundations of another Europe, a Europe of the common good for all Europeans.

Plan B and the new Treaty

In English, it's the "Reform Treaty" which sounds more upbeat than the neutral and boring French "Traité modificatif" or "Treaty which modifies". This is Plan B incarnate, the new instrument they hope to push through before anyone knows exactly what hit them and which differs barely a jot or tittle from the failed Constitution it replaces. Before we deal with its numerous complexities and the sleight of hand involved in foisting it on hapless Europeans, here is a short chronicle of post-TEC history and the state of play as of autumn 2007.

In July 2005, a further referendum took place in tiny Luxembourg where the Yes came out ahead. A jubilant

Prime Minister Juncker announced that this proved the "Constitution is not dead… it remains alive on the agenda of the European Union".[1] This reminded me of the Monty Python "dead parrot" sketch in which the pet shop manager keeps trying to convince an angry customer that his dead parrot – purchased half an hour previously – is merely resting, or hibernating, or awaiting the right moment to speak. Juncker forgot one thing: the rule was unanimity and unanimity was dead. So they had to come up with something else. The something has now been unveiled and its timeline is already set, although they didn't bother to inform us they had come up with Plan B until the meeting in Berlin in March 2007 celebrating the 50th anniversary of the founding of Europe.

I'll explain in a moment how this Treaty does – or mostly doesn't – differ from the Constitution. The basic message is, however, that the Eurocrats learned their lesson; so did national governments. As Günter Verheugen might have said: Do not, under any circumstances, allow the peoples of Europe to say anything about their future. Avoid referenda; push the next text through, with no time for discussion or debate. Leave all the anti-democratic, neo-liberal measures just as they were in the Constitution – or make them more binding – but also make sure they are even more difficult to identify and that the text is even more complicated for ordinary mortals to decipher. Make sure too that the new Treaty, once approved by governments, cannot be altered. Democracy is dangerous; it can result in incorrect decisions, but this time the outcome will be determined well in advance and the people can exercise their God-given right to shut up.

The sequence of events in 2007 leading to the Treaty was the following: The Council (heads of state and government) delivered a formal mandate to the Intergovernmental Conference (IGC) in June; the Portuguese presidency presented the IGC with a draft Treaty on 23 July; the IGC adopted the final draft on 19 October as I hand in this chapter to the publisher of this book. *

The Treaty will then be sent round for ratification by all 27 members, well in time for the European parliamentary elections in June 2009. Nearly all Member States will opt for parliamentary ratification; President Sarkozy has already announced that there will be no more of this referendum nonsense in France; there is some doubt about the method to be used in Britain, the Czech Republic, Poland and some other smaller States, eight in all. The only Member requiring a referendum by law is Ireland and this places a great responsibility on the shoulders of the Irish.

Here is the first paragraph of the mandate (I especially like the bit about "democratic legitimacy"):

The IGC is asked to draw up a Treaty (hereinafter called "Reform Treaty") amending the existing Treaties with a view to enhancing the efficiency and **democratic legitimacy** of the enlarged Union, as well as the coherence of its external action. The constitutional concept, which consisted in repealing all existing Treaties and replacing them by a single text called "Constitution", is abandoned. The Reform Treaty will introduce into the existing Treaties, which remain in force, **the innovations resulting**

* According to *Le Monde*, the head of EU legal services in charge of drafting the text is a Frenchman, Jean-Claude Piris. (*Le Monde*, 18 October 2007, special page on Europe, p. 3.)

from the 2004 IGC, as set out below in a detailed fashion.
(my emphasis)

So the negotiators have in one hand the "existing Treaties"
and in the other hand the changes made to these existing
treaties by the now defunct Constitution. Since this
Constitution is "abandoned", these changes are retained,
but cleverly disguised as "the innovations resulting from
the 2004 IGC". The "2004 IGC" is none other than the
one that approved the Constitution submitted by Giscard's
Convention and sent it out for ratification. Neat, no?

So what are the "existing treaties"? Here too, we have
to be prepared for some confusing name-changes. The text
of the IGC's mandate reads:

> The Reform Treaty will contain two substantive clauses
> amending respectively the Treaty on the European
> Union (TEU) and the Treaty Establishing the European
> Community (TEEC). The TEU will keep its present name
> and the TEEC will be called Treaty on the Functioning of
> the Union, the Union having a single legal personality.

In other words, the IGC must merge and mesh these two
existing treaties with the changes – or "innovations" –
introduced by the dead Constitution, minus a few listed
exceptions. The "existing treaties" are the **Treaty on the
European Union** (TEU, that is, the Maastricht Treaty, as
modified by the treaties of Amsterdam and Nice) and the
Treaty Establishing the European Community (TEEC, Rome
1957, plus later modifications).* The integration of these

---

* The word "Community" is to be replaced throughout by "Union".

two "existing treaties" with everything that was new and different in the Constitution minus the exceptions, means that all the provisions of the Constitution which are **not** listed are going to remain law and will figure in the Reform Treaty exactly as they appeared in the ex-Constitution. The name of the resulting new Treaty is not "Reform" in the sense of making beneficial changes. It is simply called that because it modifies (re-forms) the "existing treaties" (clearer in the French "*traité modificatif*"). Sometimes in French they dare to call it the "*Traité simplificatif*" ("which simplifies") or "*simplifié*" ("simplified"). Unfortunately it is neither: the word "*complicatif*" doesn't exist in French (though "*complexifier*" arguably could) but if it did, if would be apt. That is what the new Treaty does – it complicates.

Judge for yourself. What must be merged and meshed? There are fully 296 modifications listed in the July 2007 draft, occupying 145 pages; all these must be stuffed into various articles of the two existing treaties. The modified treaty, as duly approved by the IGC, comes to 410 articles, often extremely detailed. Twelve protocols (69 pages) and 51 declarations (63 pages) are generously appended. Declaration number 11 contains the 51 articles of the Charter of Fundamental Rights, previously Part II of the dead Constitution. A good many of the declarations explain how to interpret this Charter.* Various annexes are also part of the package and all this literature – protocols, declarations, annexes – has the same legal value as the 410-article Treaty itself.†

---

* The Charter only applies to Member States when they act in the context of EU law – otherwise the principle of subsidiarity applies and the Members determine the rights of their citizens.

† I am indebted to Francis Wurtz, a French Euro-parliamentarian from the United European Left group (GUE), to Pierre Khalfa of the

The new Treaty, whether "Modificatif" or "Reform", is everything one feared, and worse. This is extremely serious because at least 80 per cent of the legislation passed in every European country now emanates directly from Brussels – which alone shows how vital it is for European citizens to understand what is happening – otherwise, they will at some point be mugged by reality. Furthermore, not only do European Treaties take precedence over national law but the European Court of Justice has already decided and reiterated that *any* rule promulgated by the European Commission also takes precedence over national law, even over national Constitutions. In other words, whatever its name, the new Treaty, legally speaking, will be just as potent as the dead Constitution would have been.

It is impossible to analyse all the provisions but it is particularly important to understand that the way European decisions are taken varies from one area to another and that there are 177 different areas and sub-areas of competence. The Commission has the lion's share of decision-making power, particularly in the areas of trade and competition; monetary policy is made exclusively by the European Central Bank. In some areas, the Council shares responsibility for approving decisions with the Parliament; in others, it can decide by itself without parliamentary interference. Some decisions require qualified majority voting (QMV); others depend on unanimity. The Council shares responsibility – but has priority – with the Union for decisions concerning

French trade union Solidaires, and to Robert Joumard, a member of Attac, all of whom have analysed the new Treaty in record time. To help us sort out this extremely complex document I will use their observations, as well as my own, freely and interchangeably and without appending a note to each one.

the internal market, agriculture, transport, energy, security, justice and most of social and environmental policy. The Commission is said to be "complementary" to the Member States in decisions concerning the areas of health, industry, culture, tourism and education.

Qualified majority voting will apply to about 120 areas and will be more or less demanding – QMV after 2014 will require in some cases 55 per cent of the Member States (15 out of 27) and 65 per cent of the European population; in others 72 per cent of the Members (20 out of 27) and 65 per cent of the population.* Unanimity remains the rule in crucial areas like revising or amending the Treaty, fiscal policy and most aspects of social and environmental policy, not to mention foreign and defence policy.

Sorting out what decision-making mode applies to what cases is hugely complex. On the whole, the Commission emerges with its powers enhanced, the Council votes on everything whereas the European Parliament, which had little power to begin with, is still excluded from co-decision in many areas. Please do not ask me which ones: nowhere in any of the texts is there a complete list of all the areas from which the Parliament is excluded. Some of these, however, are; foreign and security policy, trade, the internal market, monetary policy, most of agricultural and social policy.

The hallowed governing principles of the separation of powers and checks and balances are forgotten if indeed they were ever remembered. The Founding Fathers of the United States felt especially strongly about these matters and set them down in the Constitution, a document of some

* However, no three Members – for example France, Britain and Germany – can block a decision even though they may have together more than 35 per cent of the population.

5,000 words. They also elaborated a Bill of Rights which has stood the test of time and even, on the whole, the test of George Bush.

On the other hand, the Charter of Fundamental Rights, first proclaimed in Nice in 2000, remains ambiguous. Understanding how the European Court might interpret it is virtually impossible, but in any case the Charter "creates no new competence or tasks for the EU" so it has little judicial value. It guarantees fewer citizens' rights than, say, the French Constitution and many other national constitutions; furthermore, no matter how weak the Charter may be, the United Kingdom has been authorised not to apply it. Ireland and Poland may follow suit. As far as one can interpret this decision, it appears to mean that while competition and market freedom are compulsory for all EU Member States, even the most meagre social rights are optional.

What is not ambiguous is the centrality of the "highly competitive internal market" that remains the supreme common denominator for the EU. Free trade also has iconic status, not just within Europe but worldwide. A new article says the goal of EU commercial policy is the "integration of all countries into the world economy... [through the suppression] of barriers to international trade". Elsewhere, it calls for the suppression of all restrictions on trade – this includes non-tariff "barriers" like environmental or consumer protection standards – as well as suppression of all barriers to foreign direct investment (FDI).

Peter Mandelson as Trade Commissioner is already putting this policy into action, notably in the EPAs or Economic Partnership Agreements he is negotiating with various countries and regions, including the very dangerous one with the 78 ACP (African, Caribbean and Pacific) countries. But the new Treaty will make the abolition of all restrictions on FDI and of "unnecessary" barriers erected by national law a permanent mandate for all future trade negotiations. External entities, like the Dispute Resolution Body of the World Trade Organisation will decide what is and is not "necessary" for consumer or environmental protection and what is a "disguised barrier to trade". The record of the WTO in this regard is not encouraging.

The European Central Bank remains independent of all political oversight and its mandate is still to maintain "price stability" (i.e. treat the smallest sign of inflation like the plague and instantly raise interest rates). For the first time, price stability becomes an "objective" of the EU; one example among many of the confusion that reigns when economic implements (like the ever-present "competition") become permanent objectives of the Union. They may be useful and desirable at some times but not others and should never share the status of genuine objective. Unanimity is still required for any limitations on the free movement of capital. This provision will almost surely be interpreted to mean that any taxes on financial transactions of the kind Attac and many other civil society organisations call for are prohibited.

European subservience to NATO for security and defence policy is reinforced. It gets a new, special protocol; the Member States signing the Treaty must promise progressively to "increase their military capabilities" (i.e. increase defence spending). The "war against terrorism" is used to justify military missions, including those organised to help *non-European* countries "combat terrorism" on their soil. We have no idea what NATO policy may be in future, but we are signing up for it blindfolded. This Treaty will never let Europe have a policy that differs from NATO's. Military cooperation between States that want to go faster and further together is specifically facilitated:

Those Member States whose military capabilities fulfil higher criteria and which have made more binding commitments to one another in this area with a view to the most demanding missions shall establish permanent structured cooperation within the Union framework.

What of the other big questions that were central to the debates and the campaign for the "No" in 2005? Neo-liberalism still rules and market freedom remains the central dogma. Charitably, we may suppose that Nicolas Sarkozy thought he was changing that model when he demanded deletion of the phrase "free and undistorted competition" from the "objectives" of the Union; he chose to call it a "major reorientation". It may be a symbolic victory for those who fought against the Constitution but under no circumstances is it a "major reorientation".

French MEP Francis Wurtz questioned Chancellor Angela Merkel (who chaired the June IGC meeting) on this point in a plenary session of the European Parliament. Her response could hardly have been more blunt: "Nothing is going to change." Not only does the phrase "free and undistorted competition" recur in the text several times but a protocol has been added which will signify "loud and clear", as Chancellor Merkel herself put it, that "this instrument [of free and undistorted competition] must be preserved in the fullest sense". Commission President Barroso, whom Wurtz also questioned, then dotted the i's and crossed the t's, replying that the principle of competition must under no circumstances be "undermined" because it is "one of the essential components of the single market. This must be crystal clear."

The Council also stressed the point in its June meeting – its paragraph concerning economic, social and environmental issues states that

> *Further strengthening* the four freedoms of the internal market (free movement of goods, persons, services and capital) and improving its functioning remain of *paramount importance* for growth, competitiveness and employment. (my emphasis)

We also campaigned in 2005 on the place of public services in Europe. Here again, nothing has changed and public services (never called that but rather "services of general economic interest") remain subject to the rules of competition. However, a protocol does specifically give national, regional and local authorities a bit more leeway than previously for supplying public services, which is welcome.

Other "innovations" retained from the Constitution include the offices of President of the Council elected for a two-and-a-half year term renewable once and a "High Representative", effectively the Foreign Minister, who deals with foreign affairs and security. The number of commissioners will be reduced and the powers of the Commission President increased. A minimum of nine Member States can decide to undertake "enhanced cooperation" among themselves in areas of their choosing.

The Union, for the first time, obtains the status of a "legal person" meaning that it can sign agreements and treaties on its own in the name of all the Member States. This could be extremely dangerous. The EU could act on its own, democratic accountability would be even further out of reach. For example, the Commission could "open" whole European service sectors to trading partners under the rules of the GATS (General Agreement on Trade in Services of the WTO). It would thus acquire a huge bargaining chip with other countries because it could "offer" a market of 450 million consumers to their exporters.

As to relations with Member States, an annex stresses that European law takes precedence over national law (with a list of the Court decisions to that effect) and national parliaments are given eight weeks rather than six to examine the legislation sent to them by the Commission and writing it into national law.

One could go on for pages more, but the main *political* points are these: The new Treaty retains virtually all of the rejected Constitution and is if anything longer and more complex. It is uniquely neo-liberal in letter and in spirit. It has been placed on the table for approval and ratification with undue haste, allowing no time for debate and it will not on the whole be submitted to referenda. It is not clear who wrote it; it seems to be the legal services of the Council. So not even an appointed Convention or similar body had a hand in it. The coalition of neo-liberals, social-liberals, EU technocrats in Brussels, transnational corporate executives, lobbyists and UNICE remains in place and can be well pleased.

But don't take my word for it: listen rather to the people who know, like Valéry Giscard d'Estaing, principal architect of the TEC. As he explained to the Constitutional Affairs Committee of the European Parliament on 17 July 2007:

As for content, the proposals are largely unchanged, they are just presented differently. This is because the new text was not supposed to look too much like the Constitutional Treaty. European governments therefore agreed on cosmetic changes [in the Reform Treaty] to make it easier to swallow....

And in the French press, the same VGE pointed out that

the [Constitutional innovations] had to be split up into several texts so they would look like simple amendments... they would be regrouped in a Treaty which had become colourless and painless. These various texts would be sent to [national] Parliaments which would vote on them separately. In that way, public opinion would be unwittingly led to adopt the provisions that [governments] didn't dare present to them straightforwardly. (*Le Monde*, 14 June 2007)

His Vice-President of the Constitutional Convention, Giuliano Amato, is also quite frank:

It was decided that the document had to be unreadable because if it's unreadable that means it's not constitutional – that was the idea.... If people could understand the text on the first reading, then you would risk getting calls for referendums....

Plenty of others agree. The Belgian foreign minister is more graphic:

The goal of the Constitutional Treaty was to be legible [readable]. The goal of this one is to be unreadable [illegible]. The aim of the Constitution was to be clear; the aim of this one is to be obscure. It is successful.

Commissioner Margot Wallstrom says simply, "It's essentially the same proposal as the former Constitution." Or Irish premier Bertie Ahern: "90 percent of the Constitution is there." The Spanish Prime Minister José Luis Zapatero waxes almost lyrical: "We have not abandoned a single essential point of the Constitution... This is without any doubt much more than a treaty. This is a fundamental, a founding document, a treaty for a new Europe."*

So it is as if the French and the Dutch had never voted. The whole process leaves all European citizens, whatever their Member State, completely out of the picture; they will have nothing to say about the way Europe runs their affairs nor about which policies should be included in the new document. The leadership is also clearly worried that citizens might still have time to get organised, so they are de facto excluding discussion of a text of supreme complexity and considerable ambiguity by pushing it quickly through the ratification process. Amendments and revisions still require unanimity, tantamount to making them impossible. The Commission will continue to hold practically all executive, legislative and even judicial power. The EU will be legally tied to the United States defence Establishment and thus to its commander in chief, the US President.

Citizens of Europe: This is your last chance.

* Thanks to Robert Joumard who compiled, in French, these and other gems in a list titled "They said it". All translations mine.

What must we do?

First, we have to go out and explain, fast, what is in this new Treaty and why it is dangerous. We have to make sure that Europeans are as worried about a "Treaty" as they were about a "Constitution" which sounds more solemn and permanent, although they have exactly the same functions and the same clout. The good side is that the word "Constitution" woke up the French, the Dutch and some other European citizens. Every journey to a different European Member State from one's own should be used to work for consensus against this European straitjacket. *We must demand an extensive inter- and intra-European debate, and referenda in every country, preferably on the same day.* Europe needs entirely new "software" in the place of the neo-liberal dogma now imposed on us.

The first requirement is obviously not to let this Treaty past the post. It would be a major victory if this could be achieved. Once Europeans understand the general orientation of the "Reform" Treaty, there are many specific points we should make sure are included in any future governing document. I shall list some of them, with the understanding that these are suggestions only; that they do not make up an exhaustive list, and that they are naturally up for debate. The main thing is that the will of the people must be sovereign and given clear, democratic paths for its expression. That popular will is in itself a concern, because so far, no "European people" exists. We have 27 peoples with different histories, languages and cultures.

All of them deserve respect and admiration because together they make the continent exceptionally rich. Why claim that the French and the Finns, the Hungarians and the

Spanish are part of a single people when each contributes to the creative diversity of the whole? We are different peoples but we also have much in common, including common aspirations to greater democracy, and together we can build the common good while maintaining our diversity. The best way to build the common good is to develop the concept of the European *citizen* and to recognise that the common good does not depend on common origins, history, language and culture. One day, perhaps Germans will feel concerned by the distress of the Andalusian unemployed and the Finns will feel affected by a strike in Belgium or Slovenia; but even if they don't today, they can recognise that they live in a common space and should have a say in developing the rules governing that space.

We need a Europe in which all Europeans feel represented but no Member State (nor the Commission) can block the progress of any other, particularly in the areas of health, education, public or social services and the environment. Citizenship, or more importantly – a people – has never flourished around an economy. No "market", whatever its size, has ever given birth to a society. Rather, a society must exist beforehand in order to determine what kind of market is appropriate, and to define marketable and non-marketable goods, public and private property. Allowing the market to impose its will on society is suicidal.

New directions, major reorientations

Two apparently simple questions should guide our thinking about new directions: Why Europe? How Europe? The answers depend on identifying goals we can reach together that none of us could reach alone, and determining the means at our disposal to achieve those goals – which may be cultural, social, political, ecological and so on.

The answer to the first question, "Why Europe?" was initially provided by the founding fathers fifty years ago and remains valid. We needed Europe first of all to bring lasting peace and make future military conflict on the continent unthinkable. For half a century, the formula has worked (the Balkans, not part of the EU, are the sad exception). Second, we needed common foundations that the main individual European countries would have a shared interest in defending. The economic foundations have indeed been laid, but with no social dimension. Crucial issues like employment and the fight against poverty and exclusion have been completely forgotten.

We needed institutions encouraging solidarity in order to develop a Europe of common interests. And here the failure is obvious. Only the Commission is recognised as capable of identifying the European "common good" and, as we know, this Commission is unelected, opaque, unaccountable and largely beholden to corporate lobbies and financial institutions. Since the ratification of the Maastricht Treaty, the Commission has been shored up by a central bank that answers to no political constituency and manages Europe as if it were a conglomerate of 27 corporations, each with its board of directors.

The "common" interest has become almost synonymous with the interest of corporations and financial markets. Social solidarity has been completely forsaken and the notorious "democratic deficit" proven time and again, by record rates of abstention among other indicators. Until the Constitutional referenda of 2005, European elections verged on the farcical. In the parliamentary elections of 2004, 54 per cent of Spaniards, 57 per cent of Germans and French, 61 per cent of the Dutch and the British, did not bother to vote. In the year that separated these elections of 2004 and the referendum of 29 May 2005, French voter participation increased by 27 points, to 70 per cent, while the Dutch doubled their turnout of 2004. When asked their opinion on matters of import, Europeans speak out.

If ordinary European elections arouse such scant interest, it is doubtless because citizens understand that their elected representatives can't do much and that an impenetrable bureaucracy is shaping Europe in their stead. When finally asked what they thought – after 13 years as was the case in France – they rejected that Europe. The fact remains that we need Europe more than ever because globalisation poses real threats and presents real challenges.

Speaking at Trinity College in Dublin, Henry Kissinger once said: "globalisation is really just another name for the dominant role of the United States". We may indeed be to a large extent under US domination, but not even the United States controls the financial mechanisms that underlie global competition, not merely between producers or workers in different places but also *between social systems*. Globalisation, or early twenty-first-century capitalism, respects only one rule: the rate of return, it deepens inequalities, irreparably harms the environment, plays havoc with cultural identities and oppresses all nations, especially the weakest. It favours the emergence of giant international and national capitalist groups in a position to impose their rules on the rest of the world.

This new reality fundamentally changes what the construction of Europe means. The bipolar post-war, Cold War world has been swept aside and replaced by a new world order built around key international economic powers, none of which is an ally of Europe, in the sense of defending common interests, especially not the United States. The belief that the United States is Europe's "friend" is a naive illusion. The key question is what role Europe wants, can and must play in this new order. This role ought not to be defined, as it has been up to now, solely by the Commission and the financial and corporate elites: the decision belongs to the peoples of Europe. We will consider Europe as a geopolitical power in the following chapter.

Policy made in Brussels and approved by Member governments since the early 1980s has had one clear thrust: the European Union has chosen to be a vehicle for neo-liberal globalisation, a market entirely open to global competition, a political entity dedicated more to breaking down social and environmental safeguards in Member States than to reinforcing them. Europe has chosen the ultra-liberal path and to follow the American lead. The clash between these two models, the European (or what's left of it) and the American, lay at the heart of the Yes–No battle because European governments of whatever persuasion have consistently chosen to follow the road that leads to the US ultra-competitive model. The European model still exists, as the final chapter will show in more detail, but is under fire from all sides.

The French economist Jean-Paul Fitoussi points out that the more an economy is globalised, the more its citizens need to be protected in order to succeed, economically or socially. Exposing Europeans simultaneously to competition internally with new Member States and externally with the US, China, India and all the others is a recipe for failure.

The Constitutional Treaty came after Maastricht, Amsterdam and Nice: all these treaties moved towards greater liberalisation of the labour market, more casual (or as the French call it "precarious") work, more "flexibility" for wages and working conditions, transformation of all human activities into commodities, privatisation of public services, destruction of the industrial base through the acceptance of cut-throat competition inside and outside Europe. The Constitution was simply one more attempt to radicalise and speed up the process.

The Reform Treaty follows the pattern. The proposal was bad as a Constitution and it's bad as a Treaty. It actually renders common European citizenship structurally impossible because Europeans are placed in unfair competition with each other and, worse still, the advanced and less advanced social systems are also made to compete against each other, with foreseeable results. In short, the blueprint is intended to turn Europe into a different continent where the norm is the war of all against all and where solidarity is the exception.

In that case, "Why Europe?" The best answer is that Europe could *potentially* become an exceptional place on earth and European peoples could achieve things together none of them could achieve alone. They could create a political entity different from a mere free trade area where rampant liberalism will eat them alive. Why bother with Europe if it's only to make it like everywhere else? The whole point should be to propose a viable alternative to neo-liberal globalisation and to prove that a different social model, indeed a different model of civilisation is possible, one that puts its trust in the common good.

As to the second question, "How Europe?" the answer lies in democracy and intergovernmental cooperation; in integrating policies and making some mild, voluntary sacrifices in the richer countries for the benefit of the poorer ones in the name of social, political, environmental and cultural European equality. What would the Treaty of our Desires look like? It would be first a framework of principles and rules (like the US Constitution which establishes the separation of powers and the checks and balances between them). These principles and rules would be, so to speak, the treasure chest while the treasure inside would be the political and social European project.

The Constitution and the "Reform" Treaty confuse the container and the thing contained by providing hugely detailed neo-liberal content and putting it in an unalterable and anti-democratic container. Our rulers are so scared that people might actually figure out what is going on that they have put the process on fast-forward and hope the ratifications will be out of the way before citizens can catch up. Nonetheless and for what they are worth, I want to outline some of the necessary elements of the European project as I see it, beginning with the framework.

The main principles

Many political principles are already, or soon could be consensual among European citizens. I've identified a dozen which take in both the "Why" and the "How" aspects of an alter-Europe project; I've also chosen to draft them in the present tense which we might call the "present tense of hope and conviction". It is understood that the text of a new Constitutional Treaty is produced by an elected Constitutional Convention whose members have full rights to propose elements of the text, as do national parliaments or a given predetermined number of petitioning European citizens. Ratification of the finished text takes place simultaneously by popular referenda in all Member States.

1. **The primary objective of the Union is the common good**. All the other objectives contribute to the common good, such as social, cultural and democratic progress, full employment, social protection, high-quality public services accessible to all, solidarity between citizens and peoples, the protection and improvement of the environment, gender equality and so on. "Competition" may sometimes be a tool to reach some of these objectives but it is always a means to an end, under certain circumstances and at particular moments. It is not an end in itself and has no place in any article of a treaty.

2. **The new treaty recognises and seeks to remedy the present severe democratic deficit in Europe**. To create a democratic Europe, the treaty carefully defines the institutions and the scope of their powers, as well as the nature of their relationships; devoting particular attention to checks and balances between the executive, legislative and judicial branches, their reciprocal responsibilities and their inbuilt capacities to prevent abuses. It further defines the rights and duties of European citizens, drawing inspiration from, among others, the Declaration of the Rights of Man and the Citizen (1789), the Universal Declaration of Human Rights (1948) and the two protocols on Civil and Political Rights and Economic, Social and Cultural

Rights (1966). It refrains from recommending specific economic policies (as Part III of the Constitution did and the Reform Treaty does).

Among necessary measures to bring about greater democracy are drastic reductions in the power of the Commission which combines executive, legislative and even some judicial powers; increased parliamentary authority – among other capacities – to levy taxes and introduce legislation as well as to remove individual commissioners from office. MEPs and commissioners from individual countries are elected by the citizens of that country (or chosen from a slate provided by the citizens of that country); the President (if one is decided upon) is elected by all European citizens in a pan-European vote, held simultaneously in the Member States. Citizens acquire genuine powers of petition, initiative and recall.

3. **Environmental sustainability, restoration and improvement are integral to all European policies and directives**. At present, directives are either hugely influenced by industry (e.g. the chemicals directive REACH) or much too weak (e.g. the protection of biodiversity). Europe also sets aside funds for R&D in the field of environmental technologies and provides adequate budgets for action in individual Member States in need as well as for cross-border environmental projects and integration.

4. **The stability pact, which places limits on public debt and inflation levels, is entirely revised**. This is not to say that no common financial rules are necessary, but so long as member countries encounter different

situations at different times, flexible and differentiated treatment is required.

5. **An alternative Europe for the common good must be able to draw on significant resources commensurate with its high ambitions**. Funding will come from various sources, demanding in turn profound changes in the current approach to European policy financing. The following observations apply:

- The European Union as well as the Euro-group acquire the capacity to borrow. This implies that, like any other government, the EU or the Euro-group can issue bonds. In the framework of enhanced cooperation, it is also possible that the Euro-group of (now) 13 European countries sharing this currency (or some of those countries), may wish to issue joint bonds. Public savings thus collected are used for large-scale public works serving the public interest (river and railway freight transport networks, ports, renewable energies...), for environmental protection and renewal, for scientific research and so on.

- The Euro-zone is the core of the EU because it can use the common currency as a political and social instrument and because it represents over three-quarters of the European population (350 of 450 million people). The euro serves the development of Europe, not private financial speculators; the interest rate reflects the needs of European businesses and of European citizens, not those of financial markets. Political choices favour either a "strong" or a "weak" euro depending on the circumstances, as is the case for most countries worldwide, particularly the United States, Japan, or China. European tax havens are placed under public administrative supervision and a uniform European corporate tax is introduced for financing EU needs. A harmonised European fiscal policy is examined and gradually implemented.

- The European Central Bank is no longer placed beyond political oversight; it reports to the Commission, to the Council and to the European Parliament. Its mandate goes beyond price stability and control over inflation in order to encompass economic growth (based on ecological principles) and full employment. The ECB's president, currently appointed for a period of nine years, can be removed from office if a majority of, say, two-thirds of the European Parliament or three-quarters of the national parliaments so decide. The Euro-group, composed of the finance ministers of the relevant Member States, share the financial and monetary management of their own area with the ECB.

- The European Union's budget is not arbitrarily fixed in the treaty at such and such a proportion of GDP but varies according to democratically established guidelines. A significant part of this budget is automatically allocated to structural funds benefiting the new Member States in order to eliminate the two-speed EU. Part of the budget comes from taxes levied by the European Parliament (notably on pollution or CO_2 and other greenhouse gas emissions).

6. **Public services are acknowledged as essential and integral to the success of the European project**. Some of these services are specific to Member States, others are progressively integrated over the whole or part of the European territory (railways, energy...). Public education, aid to young children and the elderly is free; State or European tax-financed subsidies for transport, water or energy systems are the norm; the public–private mix of various services (culture, broadcasting...) is democratically determined.

7. **In the same spirit, Europe reassesses its participation in international trade agreements**. In the case of the World Trade Organisation, the EU demands the revision of agreements such as the GATS and the TRIPS that deal with trade in services or intellectual property. In so far as possible, the EU opens its borders to the produce of poorer countries and strives to increase their involvement in global commerce on an equitable basis, according to the codified principles of "special and differential treatment". It halts subsidies to agricultural exports and focuses on its own food sovereignty and, where *locally* appropriate, on agro-fuels (the latter are not, however, the primary alternative energy source).

8. **Education and research are top priorities**. Programmes like "Erasmus" that allow young people to study in other European countries are strengthened and made compulsory. At least one European language other than one's own (which is also stressed) is compulsory from infant school. A "lifetime education credit account" is established, enabling all European citizens to take periodic sabbaticals for professional training or personal

pursuits. Fundamental and applied research is favoured in all fields and the research budget is given priority.*

9. **Enhanced cooperation is facilitated in all areas**. Member States that wish to move faster and further than others towards European objectives have the freedom to do so, so long as the cooperation remains open to new Members at all times. Neither the Commission nor other Member States unwilling to join a particular enhanced cooperation programme have a right of veto. Any cooperation undertaken between members of the Europe-15 is accompanied by contributions to the twelve (or more) countries included in successive enlargements. Certain forms of enhanced cooperation, for example in the provision of development aid, may be declared accessible to non-EU countries.

10. **The EU rapidly attains the United Nations goal of 0.7 per cent of GDP for overseas development aid (ODA) – a target set in 1974.** The Union undertakes the coordination of Member States' development aid policies, with their collaboration, in order to rationalise these policies and avoid duplication. Countries receiving this aid are no longer required to deal with individual European missions that waste personnel, time and money. ODA priority is accorded to countries bordering the Mediterranean and the ACP countries (Africa, Caribbean, Pacific).

11. **Security and defence policies are European, defined by Europeans and are not tied to any non-European structures**. All Member States cooperate in the gathering and dissemination of intelligence. Countries

---

* But the hugely complex procedures involved in obtaining EU research grants are completely overhauled: see below.

that wish to retain NATO membership may do so, but NATO is not recognised as a European organisation endowed with decision-making powers capable of affecting European choices, nor can NATO members risk involving Europe in wars. Europe as a geopolitical power is not dependent on militarisation and no treaty can force an EU Member State to increase its military capabilities or arms expenditures. "Security and defence" are not seen as purely military matters but depend also on maintaining good cooperative relations with other States and on the development of peace-keeping forces, which are in themselves deterrents to conflict (see following chapter).

12. **All treaty texts can be revised**. Amendment and revision are important steps not to be undertaken lightly, but they must be possible. A certain proportion of Member State parliaments, in combination with a certain percentage of the Euro-Parliament should be able to propose amendments which give rise to a popular consultation in all Member States on the same day. Amendments become law through qualified majority voting of both parliamentary and popular majorities, pegged to a high standard (two-thirds? three-quarters?).

Some specifics

Since the TEC and the Reform Treaty completely gloss over these issues, it is reasonable to bring them up here. Many of them need fundamental rethinking. Here, in my view, are a few of them.

Re-examine the Charter of Fundamental Rights. This document, now removed from the Treaty proper and placed in a declaration, is supposed to be "solemnly proclaimed" the day the new Treaty is ratified. As already noted, it creates "no new tasks or obligations for the Union" and is extremely weak and regressive compared to many national constitutions. It does not provide the "right to work" or "to have work" in the sense of a right to a job or of compensation when unemployed (unemployment is not mentioned anywhere in the Treaty). It simply means you can work if you can find a job. The right to social protection is reduced to "access to social security allocations and social services", with no mention of their quantity or quality. The right to contraception and abortion is not guaranteed and health rights in general are left extremely vague. You have the right to marry and to have a family, but not specifically to divorce. No right to a minimum income nor to a pension is mentioned. It would seem no accident that the European Union is not party to the 1948 Universal Declaration of Human Rights of the United Nations; only to the far weaker European Convention of 1950 which does not mention any collective or social rights.

Overhaul trade policy. The European Trade Commissioner negotiates for all 27 Member States, whether in the World Trade Organisation or in bilateral and regional trade agreements. Over the past decade, this commissioner (beginning with Leon Brittan, then Pascal Lamy, now Peter Mandelson) has acted solely in the interests of corporations and worked to place firmly all human activities in the marketplace, including education, health, culture, research, water and public services.

An estimated 15,000 lobbyists are busy exerting influence for their clients in Brussels, but when corporate lobbies do not exist, the Commission sends out an SOS to transnational corporations to organise one; as Leon Brittan did when he realised that Europe, unlike the US, had no organised services lobby. He seems to have rung up some banker friends in London and invited or incited them to create the European Services Forum, which currently includes over eighty European transnationals in various branches of activity. The Trade Directorate models its negotiating stance on the preferences of these corporations.

Attac-France and other European NGOs have campaigned particularly against the General Agreement on Trade in Services, one of the most dangerous WTO instruments, and they have successfully brought over a thousand local and regional governments to declare themselves "GATS-free Zones". These successes, although symbolic rather than legally binding, should be built upon and a new Services agreement protecting national preferences and public services drafted. Regional agreements – in which Europe is invariably the stronger partner – must also be overhauled to protect the peoples of less-developed countries. Ideally, we should declare the Doha Round of the WTO dead and start rethinking the whole trade universe. Many groups have concrete proposals about a more equitable world trade regime.

Reorient agriculture and fisheries policy. Fishing rights are granted at present on a political basis, regardless of the ecological and biological consequences. European industrial trawlers have stripped African coastal fisheries clean; Europeans are then surprised when former fishermen use their boats to transport potential migrants to the Canaries or the Italian islands.

The Common Agricultural Policy (CAP) favours a "productivist", high-capital-input form of agriculture to the detriment of the environment, and it showers the wealthier farmers with subsidies while driving smallholders to bankruptcy. The Commission has declared that no State can outlaw genetically modified organisms (GMOs) once and for all. The CAP also contributes to ruining producers in the South by continuing to subsidise European exports (and Europeans are then, once more, surprised when former farmers take enormous risks to emigrate). Present policy looks to "increased productivity" but says nothing about maintaining rural communities and employment nor about environmental and rural habitat protection. A new policy should aim for food sovereignty, increased help for small, specialised farmers, development of bio-production and an end to GMOs and to exports destructive to farmers elsewhere.

Encourage "enhanced cooperation". Though not impossible under present rules, enhanced cooperation between Member States is hemmed about with obstacles and at least a third of those States (9 out of 27) must agree in order to undertake any cooperation or harmonisation of policy. This is doubtless also due to the Commission's heavy bias in favour of privatisation and "competition", making cooperation in, say, the fields of energy and transport particularly difficult so as to leave the free market free to do its work. European successes like Airbus or Ariane (geo-satellites) are private ventures, not the product of official European industrial policy. So long as the Commission retains veto power over similar, public ventures, these will undoubtedly not happen. Enhanced cooperation ought to be a lot more flexible and adaptable, allowing each country to move at its own pace without having to violate popular will in the name of "European obligations". These cooperations would of course be open to all, at any time.

Finance enhanced cooperation. When the PIGS (Portugal, Ireland, Greece, Spain) joined Europe, structural funds were set aside to bring them quickly up to scratch compared to the existing Members – a policy which, on the whole, worked extremely well. Nothing of that scope exists for the ten, now twelve newcomers – they are instead being maintained as reservoirs of cheap labour and sites for outsourcing. Enhanced cooperation should be accompanied by a small self-imposed tax through which the participating countries tax themselves in order to bring the weaker countries to the same level. Otherwise, these weaker members will continue to see such cooperation as a mechanism to enrich the rich while leaving the others to stagnate. Other financing methods are also possible: see below.

For progressives, specific political realities plead in favour of creating a fair and level playing field for the twelve new members: most of them vote for the right or the extreme right and will continue sending rightists to Parliament and the Commission unless they have good reason to change. In the 2004 Euro-Parliamentary elections, only 26 per cent of new Member State voters turned out and three-quarters of those who bothered to vote did so in favour of the traditional right (51 per cent) and the extreme right (21 per cent). For the moment, they are scarcely thinking at all in European terms; they concentrate rather on narrow national interests (such behaviour is not, of course, confined to the new members and Britain deserves special mention here).

A successful alternative Europe project: the major challenges

Within the framework of the twelve principles listed above we can now more fully define the content of the European project we want and examine the main challenges we face. Here is a quick overview. The challenge of making Europe a genuinely geostrategic power is discussed in the next chapter.

The most urgent problem is undoubtedly to halt and reverse the growing gap between rich and poor Europeans, the "winners" and "losers"; the "ins" and the "outs"; a trend linked to instability and to the upheaval of the social and employment models won by peoples' movements especially since the Second World War.

A Europe based on the supremacy of competition and the all-powerful market is an Americanised Europe. This is not by accident but by design. An environment of precarious or casual work is ideal for capital, allowing it to adjust labour and production as needed whenever it likes. This situation then begins to feed on itself and on the despair of people ready to work at any price. An extreme example occurred in Germany where a given job would be auctioned off to the lowest bidder – in terms both of salary and acceptance of working conditions most beneficial to the employer. The law of the jungle takes over, except that this statement is unfair to animals. Ethology tells us that animals are generally more willing than humans to cooperate with each other in such situations.

The classic Marxist equation of "capital versus labour" no longer fully applies. Nor are we still entirely in the euphemistic framework of "social partners", that is, employers and trade unions. Social partners is still the code phrase used in Brussels but Europe is gradually evolving towards a situation more reminiscent of the nineteenth century, when unionised workers were far fewer and the "reserve labour army" was growing and begging to be exploited. Organised social regression is central to neo-liberal globalisation and to the present European project as designed by the elites.

We have a choice between the American way of labour market "flexibility" and the European way, even though it is becoming less and less feasible in the neo-liberal straight-jacket which will, if allowed, spell the end of the European social model. To retain and preserve it, our only available strategy resides in more cohesion and demand for social protection across the board. We will not be able to maintain this protection much longer in individual countries, even the large ones like France, Germany or Britain, where it is under constant attack. The strategy becomes virtually impossible in a Europe of 25 or 27 countries with widely diverging standards.

Enlargement of Europe is an accomplished fact and cannot be undone, so let us try to make the most of it so that the newcomers prosper. At the same time, citizens of "old Europe" are also suffering and under pressure and cannot reasonably be expected to compete with both the low wages of new fellow-Europeans and with the Chinese, the Indians, etc. This impossibility and the disunity it engenders are exactly what neo-liberals count on to annihilate the European social model once and for all.

To escape such a scenario, we need immediate enhanced cooperation schemes in order to protect employment, wages and social rights, with the simultaneous objective of helping new Europeans quickly to reach the same level as the older ones. Such cooperation is possible even under the Nice Treaty, even under the "Reform" Treaty if we have the misfortune to be governed by it. Neither makes enhanced cooperation easy, but the Euro-group could, for example, decide to form the social core of Europe; or, if all the Euro-States do not want to join, then France, Germany and Benelux et alia could at least set it in motion.

Since it seems unlikely that we can immediately loosen the stranglehold of the European Central Bank, some countries could make a collective bond issue to be devoted to the environmental transformation of Europe and investment in rapid development and deployment of environmental technologies. Other employment-creating infrastructure projects like those mentioned above could also reinvigorate Europe's productive capacity. Part of the return on such investment should then go to structural improvements in the newer Member States.

Another task ahead is "social harmonisation" which, in the TEC and the Reform Treaty, can only be decided unanimously – meaning, for all practical purposes, never – or only harmonisation downwards. The richer countries could start a social cohesion fund for the poorer ones to which the latter would have access on the condition that they accept certain rules and gradually dismantle their comparative advantage based on social, fiscal and wage dumping. Put differently, the original Members must make the idea of an alternative Europe sufficiently tempting to the newcomers for them to make a few short-term sacrifices, with the prospect of much larger rewards later on. It seems hardly worth building a new Europe unless European peoples benefit.

A remedy for de-industrialisation and the absence of new leading-edge industries is another important challenge linked to the European scientific research crisis and the debilitating scientific brain drain. Few Europeans know that 400,000 of their best minds, trained in their best schools, at their expense, have settled in the United States, three-quarters of them permanently. Forty per cent of the scientists now working in the United States were born in Europe. This haemorrhage can only be stanched by investing massively in research and making European laboratories and salaries attractive to high-level scientists.

The EU's present rigid research requirements do not provide the best of environments to achieve this. If you ask scientists about their experiences with the research directorate, they will tell you that either a member of their team deals exclusively with the mounds of paperwork demanded or that they decided not to make that sacrifice and consequently allowed another lab they know to be inferior to their own get the contract and the funds. Rather than trying to cover every possible contingency beforehand, Brussels should opt for giving funds to recognised scientific teams and assessing them later, on their results. I doubt the percentage of failures and wrong choices would be any greater than with the present approach. Enhanced cooperation between national scientific research councils is also an avenue to be explored but the main goal is to simplify present Kafkaesque procedures.

All R&D can be adapted and seek to build on existing strengths in various fields, but Europe should concentrate on creating centres of excellence throughout the Union – say a large centre for stem cell biology in Germany or Spain; an astronomy cluster in Italy or France, and so on. The main point is to build strong, multi-European-national centres that attain critical mass in leading edge disciplines. European scientists know perfectly well who the top people are in their own field all over Europe. The point is to reduce the bureaucratic hindrances so that they can freely and fruitfully work together, in both basic and applied research.

The United States spends twice as much as Europe on research while benefiting meanwhile from the quality of European universities that send so many of their best trained people across the Atlantic. The Chinese and the Indians are making spectacular progress in research and high-level technology. None of these rivals will show us any mercy. We must double our research and innovation budget and offer financial and fiscal incentives to start-up companies in high-tech sectors.

Another challenge involves the countries closest to the EU, starting with the countries of the Mediterranean Basin and those of Sub-Saharan Africa. The situation could quickly get out of hand if we do not soon change our policy towards them and cooperate more. How can we improve our relations with poorer countries, contribute to their development and preserve their increasingly fragile environments? These are the urgent issues. In addition to the standard call for development aid at 0.7 per cent of GDP, we need to think far more seriously about the root causes of immigration which is presently dealt with entirely in the police-security-legal context. Europe has avoided any honest examination of the *reasons* for mass migrations. People only leave their own countries, their families, their languages, their friends, their childhoods... in such overwhelming numbers when they have no alternative – particularly knowing, as they do, that they may die in the attempt to reach Europe and that, if they are lucky enough to survive the journey, they will face racism, discrimination, dirty jobs, a clandestine life without papers, and so on.

By "honest examination" I mean an assessment of the contribution European policies themselves make to closing off all avenues *except* that of migration by reducing opportunities locally. Among the policies that make migration seem a viable alternative is, most important of all, the debt accumulated by these countries and the chaos and dislocation caused by the World Bank/IMF structural adjustment ("austerity") policies that have come with it. Cancelling debt (along with measures guaranteeing that the savings are not squandered) could make a big contribution to local development and employment. An end to agricultural dumping and overfishing by European firms; paying fair prices for southern exports and a refusal to support tyrannical and corrupt regimes could do more to stem out-migration than all the police forces Europe can muster.

Concerning the immigrant populations already settled in Europe, the most urgent task is clearly to put an end to ghettos. These outer- or inner-city neighbourhoods must be made more attractive with the help of their inhabitants, who know their own needs better than anyone else. Self-determined improvement projects could provide impressive numbers of jobs and build skills but the pump must first be primed. Plenty of good ideas and pilot projects already exist in this area.

Why not develop a programme for the youngest children, immersing them from the age of two or three in the language of the country they live in. In France, some young people from immigrant neighbourhoods can leave high-school with an active vocabulary of only a few hundred words. No one can be successful in complex societies when so poorly equipped to cope.

This brief list of challenges is far from exhaustive. Two other subjects of special significance – in particular preserving a planet which cannot take any greater strain, and the nature of work and the European employment model – are topics of the two final chapters.

Confronting these challenges within the framework of the major principles set forth above is exactly the same as building a Europe of the common good. Only citizens can make this happen by demanding a Treaty which allows them to break free from the constraints that prevent such democratic, economic and social progress. European public opinion must insist that their elected representatives define themselves with regard to the principles and the project. They cannot be counted on to do so spontaneously. The whole point of saying "No" is not to refuse Europe itself but to create the shock and the political space necessary so that we can start creating the Europe we want.

Eventually, I hope that Europe will be mature enough to elect a proportionally representative constituent Assembly or Convention that can draft a genuine Constitution in an open and transparent way. But first we are faced with the urgent task of preventing the "Reform" Treaty from becoming the instrument of iron European neo-liberal rule.

Allow me to close this chapter on a personal note. I believe in Europe and I want to contribute to building it, but only if it embodies a credible project for a civilisation worthy of the history and the genius of European peoples – finally liberated from the horrors of internecine wars, mass slaughter, colonial imperialism and other unsavoury attributes of their past. I will oppose, in contrast, any text that serves only the interests of transnational corporations, the financial elites and their neo-liberal allies. History is what we make it, so those who want to help build a Europe of the common good, no matter what their national citizenship, had better start now.

4
Europe as a Geopolitical Power

Can Europe be a geopolitical and strategic power and influence the world's destiny, just as the United States, China, India, Russia or a future Asian, South-American or African federation might do? Should it be such a power? I believe the answer to both questions is Yes. Europe has a unique model and a set of values to offer the world and like any other political entity it also has interests to defend. It further has the right and the duty to build a European space on the foundations of this model, those values and those interests, involving whenever possible all the members of the Union.

In cases where not all members wish to participate, the European space can be built on enhanced cooperation. The term is used in official documents and designates a political arrangement open at any time to all EU members and sometimes to non-EU countries, like Russia, which took a positive position against the war in Iraq and whose attitude was valuable to European countries unwilling to follow the American lead. The Reform Treaty requires that at least a third of the Member States (meaning nine today) agree to join in an enhanced cooperation.

Europe's political, social and cultural model can pose "the threat of a good example" to other powers. All EU member countries are now democracies with solid executive, legislative and judicial institutions and Europe also has a tradition of social protection and intergenerational solidarity. Although its environmental record is far from exemplary, it still surpasses that of, say, the United States or China. After sixty years without intra-State conflict, we can safely say that peace is now secure within European borders, and the whole world envies our rich historical and cultural heritage. The main tourist destinations for well-off non-Europeans are Paris, London, Rome, Berlin, Madrid and now Prague, Budapest...

How can we build on these foundations to create a superpower-Europe that will work towards the common good of its own people and of the world? Let me first clear up a misunderstanding that often surfaces as soon as the subject of Europe as a geostrategic power comes up. Aiming for geopolitical power is not the same as calling for a militarised Europe, but this begs some important questions. How best to combine military strength and political influence? Who should determine security and defence policy? How much importance (and money) should be allocated to security and defence relative to other European needs? Is the American interventionist and militarist approach the only model for a geopolitical entity that intends to make a difference on the international scene?

The proposals of the Economic Defence Council

The French Economic Defence Council (Conseil Economique de la Défense, from now on CED) has formulated one possible answer to these questions. Established in 2003 at the initiative of then-Defence Minister Michèle Alliot-Marie, the nine-member CED is supposed to act as a super advisory board, reflecting on security issues, making proposals and communicating its message to a broader audience. Most of the members are military brass or military industry executives, with the addition of a mainstream classical economist, the president of the French export credit guarantee agency and a former EU Commissioner, now a corporate executive at Suez.

The CED is somewhat akin to a US-style think tank and an outsider cannot be sure of its real influence. It is clear, however, that its membership (and its long and impressive list of national and international consultants) reflects the cream of the "techno-elites". Its three working groups can call on a range of high officials in the ministries, parliament, the corporate and financial worlds, the universities and the media. One of its missions is to "convince regional, national and European opinion and those outside the defence establishment of the need for, and legitimacy of a strong defence policy".[1] The CED also seems to have contributed to the drafting of the European Constitution, as we shall see in a moment.

Alliot-Marie made public the 2005 CED report (*The Defence Economy 2005*) at a high-level seminar held at the Ecole Militaire in early June 2005. A preview of the report's conclusions appeared in the *Financial Times*, stressing the CED's recommendation that Europe increase its military spending by €45 billion yearly in order to reach 2 per cent of European GNP. Otherwise, says the CED, Europe would lag far behind the United States.[2]

Only France and the United Kingdom now spend 2 per cent of GNP on defence (compared to 3.8 per cent in the United States). If the other 23 member countries (not counting recently acceded Bulgaria and Romania) were to imitate them, the "missing" €45 billion would fall into the eager hands of the military. Altogether, Europeans now spend only a third as much as the Pentagon on military equipment, and only a fifth as much on military research.

The CED report calls on Europeans to put their divisions (over Iraq in particular) behind them and cooperate much more consistently with the United States in all areas of defence within the framework of NATO. In sum, the CED's recommendations are uncannily close to the articles of the Constitution which put Europe under NATO command and required increased military expenditure.

The nine wise men of the CED think of Europe as a future military superpower. Their earlier 2004 Report is serious, documented and technical but also in some respects methodologically embarrassing, even surreal. Before accepting that one's country ought to commit to higher military spending, wouldn't the average citizen want to know why? In France, the military budget already amounts to nearly 15 per cent of public spending (including military pensions). If Europe is supposed to come up with an extra €45 billion, which is to say a whopping 28 per cent increase in defence spending for 25 Member States, wouldn't it be reasonable to ask a few basic questions? Questions like "What for?", "Who is the enemy?", "What threats are we likely to face?" "How have these threats escalated to the extent that European taxpayers must make an unprecedented financial effort and put the continent on a virtual war footing?" "Are the military means proposed likely to reduce these threats?"

We the Peoples of Europe

Theoretically, the authors of the CED report should be able to respond to such questions since their recommendations call for extremely sophisticated weapons systems; often "systems of systems" to use their own terminology. Normally one would expect to learn against whom, or what, these systems might eventually be used. Unfortunately, our theoretical average citizen is not going to get much out of the CED on such subjects. The 2004 report says:

> The threats are evolving and diffuse, they are internal and external [...]; they call for innovative and varied responses whilst not abandoning traditional defence needs and our interest in [maintaining] interoperability with the United States.

Or, more poetically:

> There are no longer threats at our frontiers; but nor are there frontiers to our threats.

Writing like this and designating threats as "internal" or "diffuse" – thus by definition shifting and elusive, possibly posed by horrid terrorists on one's own soil – can justify just about any expense one cares to set and this is indeed how these gentlemen defend the notion that we must match American technological developments. In their 2005 report, the same CED authors emphasise the security objective of protecting supply, transport, production and distribution of oil and gas. Europe is particularly vulnerable when it comes to energy and its dependency in this sector is permanent. Fair enough: protection of energy supplies can be seen as a legitimate security need. But this factor alone cannot justify or explain the military effort demanded. "Systems of systems" are also totally ineffective for stopping people from setting off bombs in oil refineries – or in buses and trains for that matter.

Another passage in the 2004 report bears a striking resemblance to the Constitution:

> Europe's defence and weapons build-up must allow us to strengthen the European pillar of the Atlantic alliance which remains the foundation of our collective security. (CED 2004 report)

Now the Constitution:

> Commitments and cooperation in this area [of defence] shall be consistent with commitments under the North Atlantic Treaty Organisation, which, for those States which are members of it, remains the foundation of their collective defence. (I-41, 7)

The Constitution also required the Member States to "progressively [...] improve their military capabilities" (I-41, 3).[3]

Suppose Europeans are willing to make huge financial and other sacrifices and accept that the vastly increased military budget will need to be offset by reduced spending in other areas in order to reach the desired level of 2 per cent of GNP: would they actually obtain any strategic compensation or advantages for superpower Europe in return? The CED authors, with admirable candour, reply "No, none at all." They acknowledge that the United States would not relinquish an iota of its dominant position and the EU's hands would, more than ever, be tied.

> The call to Europeans to increase their [military] capabilities will not necessarily be synonymous with an increase in their room for manoeuvre [...]. The United States has clearly shown the will to increase its power within the Alliance, and consequently over Alliance members' defence policies.

In other words, NATO makes the decisions, and inside NATO, the US. Not to worry: we are all brave little Atlantic Alliance soldiers, unfailing allies of the United States; ready to pay its bills however outrageous and however much it may choose to manipulate us, or rather "increase its power... over [our] defence policies".

Despite their breathtakingly clear view of this state of affairs in 2004, a year later the same authors have become even more eager boot-lickers. Their programme for "transatlantic partnerships" assumes that Europe is passionately keen on supplying the Pentagon, despite repeated proof that the United States defence Establishment isn't interested. The 2005 CED report itself informs us that "the track record of transatlantic partnerships is modest and it seems futile to expect any loosening of the rules and regulations governing relations between the United States and Europe". What's more, they are aware that the US systematically erects legal barriers to prevent Europeans from gaining access to defence technology and markets.

Despite all this, they urge Europe to consent to "solidarity on principle between all European countries and practical solidarity between industrial groups and official

European bodies that wish to develop such partnerships". Let us set off together to take part in the great American adventure. European industries that want to sell in the US will of course have to "set up research and development centres and production units [...] on American soil [...]; the limited outcome of forty years of transatlantic partnership should not, however, lend itself to ultimate and definitive pessimism". So Onwards and Upwards. The profits, if they materialise, will go to our transnational corporations; the jobs and the fruits of our research to the Americans.

I'm dumbfounded, though grateful, that an official group attached to the French Defence Ministry could publish a document laying out precisely the European "Road to Serfdom" as Friedrich von Hayek might have put it. The CED has produced a blueprint for complete European capitulation to American interests and for a society based on militarisation – not exactly what millions of pro-Europe Europeans have dreamed about – whether they were in favour of the TEC or not.

Furthermore, the CED never seems to notice the contradiction between the terrorist threat, which everyone recognises, and the implementation of strategic measures designed for a bygone era of inter-State conflict. As soon as the Americans increase their military expenditure in any particular domain, the CED intends to rush to their side.

The Council gives the figures showing how asymmetrical the United States and Europe are. Europe represents 155 per cent of the population of the United States, 102 per cent of their GDP, but only 45 per cent of their total defence budget and 18 per cent of their military research. These numbers are apparently provided to make us feel ashamed.

For the sake of argument, however, let's assume that EU member governments unanimously adopt the recommendations of the CED and somehow find the extra €45 billion to put us on a more equal footing with the US. Big deal. Given that in 2004 the American defence budget reached €351 billion and that the defence budget of all 25 European countries combined amounted to €160 billion, adding €45 billion would bring us to €205 billion, or 59 per cent of the American budget in 2004 which has since increased. Achieving this unremarkable goal would nonetheless imply drastic cuts in expenditure for social services, research, infrastructure, education, health, culture and who knows what else.

And all this to defend ourselves against whom, or what? Have the United States and the United Kingdom, which boast the two largest military budgets in the world, been spared from terrorist attacks? Quite the contrary, their military adventurism has supplied a magnet for terrorism. The dead bodies of Afghani and Iraqi civilians are not unconnected to those in New York or London, even though they are less important to the Americans or the British in power. Pointing this out is in no way to "justify" terrorism, which is unjustifiable; it is, however, an attempt to assess rationally its motives in hopes of finding the most efficient ways to fight and eliminate it. Most Europeans would assume that diplomacy and intelligence-gathering are more effective than sophisticated equipment and quasi-colonial wars of occupation.

Europeans, and particularly the French CED authors, should also refresh their memories. Not long ago, the United States dragged the Soviet Union into an endless arms race, to the point that the USSR, unable to bear the costs, exited history. Assuming Europeans devoted 2 per cent of GNP to military budgets, we would still "lag behind" and we would not be better protected – arguably much less so. Our capacity to act independently worldwide through military or non-military means would not be enhanced but hampered by the heightened American capacity to manipulate us within NATO. We would build the walls of our own prison.

Can anyone really believe that the United States is our "partner", our "friend"? That they love and admire us and have our best interests at heart? General de Gaulle would be appalled, he who wisely said, "States have no friends – only interests." The American interest is to have no rivals, not even regional ones, nor in any sphere, particularly in military matters. Those who remain unconvinced should refer to the works of Paul Wolfowitz, who explained this doctrine clearly in 1992 in his then-secret report *Defense Planning Guidance*.

Power and weakness: Robert Kagan's analysis

Robert Kagan provides a far more realistic approach to the power relationship between the US and Europe. A doughty neoconservative (like his father and his brother), Kagan co-founded the "Project for a New American Century" in 1997 with many other rightwing luminaries who later held influential positions in the Bush administration. Kagan was once a speechwriter for George Schultz, Reagan's secretary of state; his wife was an advisor to Dick Cheney and he has all the credentials of an FPI (foreign policy intellectual) along the lines of a Samuel Huntington or a Francis Fukuyama. He knows Europe well, has lived and for all I know still lives in Brussels and unlike some American foreign policy wonks, he does not despise Europeans.[4]

Kagan also has intimate knowledge of the American national defence Establishment's views and he asks that we "stop pretending that Europeans and Americans share a common view of the world, or even that they occupy the same world". They don't, and their vision of what constitutes power increasingly differs. Americans are from Mars – named for the god of war; Europeans are from Venus, where laws, rules, negotiation and cooperation take precedence over *Machtpolitik* – the politics of strength or force. For Kagan, Europeans live in a "post-historical paradise" of peace and prosperity – the era of perpetual peace Kant described two centuries ago. Meanwhile, the United States remains bogged down in History, in the world not of Kant but of Thomas Hobbes where there is no faith in law, where one must wage the war of all against all and always be ready to unsheathe the sword.

Europeans and Americans agree less and less on fundamentals. This is no passing phase. Threats are not perceived in the same way on both sides of the Atlantic, priorities and policies diverge and there is no common "strategic culture". Europeans are frightened of an America that resorts to force at a moment's notice, scorns diplomacy and sees the world divided into black and white, good and evil, friends and foes. The Europeans' world is more complex, they prefer the carrot to the stick and work to create commercial and economic ties. Americans look for ultimate solutions and want to eliminate threats, by unilateral means if need be, with no regard for "international law", of which they are profoundly sceptical.

Kagan compares present American and European views to the ones they held in the eighteenth and nineteenth centuries. When America was a minor power, it behaved exactly as Europe does today, whereas Europeans were then constantly embroiled in *Machtpolitik* and wars – fitting pursuits for the great powers of the day. It was then in the interests of the United States, as it is in those of Europe today, to shape a world where military might was less important than institutions enforcing international rules and where all nations, large and small, strong and weak, could claim equal rights.

Europe's new "civilising mission" – as the French called their colonial adventures – is perhaps an attempt to transmit the "European miracle" of peace to the rest of the world. If the German lion and the French lamb can lie down together, anything is possible, even beyond European borders. The US insistence on operating unilaterally is a direct threat to this new European ideal and invalidates it, much as the European monarchies implicitly denied the American republican ideal in the eighteenth and nineteenth centuries. "Americans ought to be the first to understand that a threat to one's beliefs can be as frightening as a threat to one's physical security", writes Kagan. He is referring to Europe but one could well say the same for the Muslim world.

The fact remains that Europe can only pursue its Kantian vision because America is willing to take on the Kim Jong-ils and the ayatollahs of this world, just as it accepted the burden of defending Europe against the USSR during the Cold War. Europe was able to develop the European Community after the Second World War because it was sheltered by the American shield; its present policies once depended on the presence of American forces on its soil. "American power made it possible for Europeans to believe that power was no longer important", but their journey into post-history depended on the Americans staying behind.

According to Kagan, "[Europe] has become dependent on America's willingness to use its military might to deter or defeat those around the world who still believe in power politics"; those who are not post-modern but live in modern or pre-modern areas. The European paradise depends on American power deployed in a dangerous world; while access to paradise is denied the Americans precisely because they accept the fact and the burden that goes with it.

The more they are freed from military commitments, the more confident Europeans become in the effectiveness of their methods for dealing with international problems, especially since the disappearance of the Soviet Union. They believe that the transition towards the rule of law they have achieved can work even in States like Libya, Iraq or Iran. The mission Europe wants to carry forward has no need of sovereign military power.

Many Europeans would judge Kagan's portrayal of the European "paradise" as too angelic by half and correctly point to examples like France's support for (and sometimes participation in) brutal military actions in its former African colonies. Kagan does tend to construct "ideal types", but he also highlights the different ways of exercising power and helps us to understand that tension and misunderstanding between America and Europe are not going to evaporate any time soon.

America will act unilaterally when it sees fit and Europe will not be able to do anything about it. In 2002, Kagan predicted exactly what would happen during and after the Iraq war – America would not take Europe's views any more seriously than those of, say, ASEAN or the Andean Pact and couldn't care less about "paradise".

The Economic Defence Council, incapable of such an analysis, stubbornly persists in believing that it is possible and useful to seek a "transatlantic partnership" at any cost, even though such a "deal" would require total surrender to America for the foreseeable future. It would be a humiliating "junior partnership", not a relationship of equals – and there is no evidence the Americans would accept it even on those terms.

Europe would increase its military spending to obtain the good graces of Big Brother across the Atlantic, but in vain. The United States, like the Trojan seer in the *Iliad* "fears the Greeks, even [some translations say 'especially'] when they bring gifts". No Trojan horses, even tame ones, for the Americans: they would accept Europeans only under firm control, if then. Various forces in Europe, especially in Britain, hope for just such an outcome and the CED and its allies will be busy betraying the Gaullist vision in order to help them. Let us hope that the French in particular and Europeans in general ignore their advice and concentrate their energies on developing the European project itself and – yes – on spreading peace and prosperity to the rest of the world whether Robert Kagan believes it possible or not.

Our real needs

The European Union, like any other power that intends to play a global role, needs a defence system. This much is obvious, just as it is obvious that its military forces should be merged in order to avoid wastefulness and reduce total, and individual Member State military spending. A

European Defence Agency has been operating since January 2005 with the mission of coordinating European military efforts and eliminating overlaps and incompatibilities. The CED, well aware of this, sees this Agency as a "body to federate European [military] cooperation programmes", for operations, research and equipment. Their obsession with transatlantic partnerships is an ideological obstacle placed in the way of a European entity able to make at least a start towards independent collective security.

To determine rationally an acceptable level of military expenditure, the best way is to start with the simple questions we posed initially. What for? Against what threats? Who are the enemies? The worst way would be to take uncritically the advice of outfits like the CED with their blatantly pro-American, militaristic bias and their total lack of interest in the social and political consequences of increased defence outlays. Europe must define the risks it faces and evaluate precisely the CED's asinine "evolving and diffuse, internal and external threats".

The next step is to act together with anyone who is willing to stand against waste, stupidity and blind militarism. Enhanced cooperation would doubtless be the easiest and most efficient method; any EU Member State could join at any time. The other defence imperative is to reduce our external energy dependency (see the following chapter on the environment).

If we could carry out these tasks satisfactorily, we could undoubtedly reduce excessive military spending – a laudable goal, but one always met with the valid objection that thousands of jobs would be destroyed. Taking France as an example, the national military budget includes €6 billion worth of government weapons and equipment procurement.

This in turn represents fully two-thirds of all government contracts, civilian or military, 180,000 people working to fulfil those contracts, and more than 260,000 soldiers and civilians paid directly from the defence budget, not counting their families or pensioners. Clearly, sudden and drastic cuts would cause an upheaval bordering on a revolution. The armed forces would not be amused.

Nonetheless, increases in the defence budget like those President Jacques Chirac regularly imposed are crazy. The CED 2005 Report provides tables showing defence spending for 31 countries. Unsurprisingly, the United States leads the list with €1,185 per capita per year, followed by the UK (€603) and France (€543). Of these 31 countries – 25 EU members plus Turkey, Russia, China, Japan, Canada and the US – 22 spend less than €300; 26 less than €400 per person.[5] With better planning and a rational, European-wide integration of forces and equipment, there is no reason we could not seriously reduce military spending without sacrificing the population's security and well-being – quite the contrary since there would be more to spend on social programmes, education and so on.

For the first time in history, EU members have known a conflict-free period of six decades, making Europe a credible force for promoting peace beyond its borders. The Union has already begun developing a rapid deployment force, available to the United Nations for intervention in conflict zones and for assistance in cases of natural or man-made disasters. Obviously we need an efficient, integrated, Europe-wide intelligence system. Police and military cooperation is vital for fighting terrorism and in this area at least we should collaborate with the United States and with non-European countries who wish it.

Why not develop European task-forces to fight against certain categories of human scum like traffickers in immigrants, women and children whose activities have reached a scale the separate police and coast-guard forces cannot cope with alone. Europeans must also develop democratically a common immigration policy, recognising for the first time how much their own policies have contributed to immigration pressures. Among the policies that incite people massively to flee their own countries are debt and structural adjustment, unfair trade, agricultural dumping, European overfishing of African waters, support for dictators... In applying a policy jointly, EU governments must also keep in mind that a Europe without immigrants would have an irredeemably aged, less dynamic population (the average European is over 40). All these issues require public debate and far greater public involvement.

We should have no illusions that the present costly and fragmented military system will change rapidly or that change will occur without a long and difficult process, but we can at least point to the innumerable advantages change would entail. We could experiment with the conversion of weapons industries to peacetime uses – the entire world managed this after the Second World War and the world's needs are at least as great today. We also have a model in the struggle of the British Lucas Aerospace workers three decades ago. When their plant was threatened with closure, the staff worked cooperatively to develop impressive, innovative products for public services and private use that they could manufacture without major new investment or costly equipment. Military industry workers today surely have as much imagination, ingenuity and expertise as these precursors. Such programmes could also begin to address the serious research and development deficit from which Europe suffers, as well as stimulating non-military high-tech product exports, particularly in environmental technologies; thus bolstering our high-tech trade balance, currently in freefall. It is up to us to demonstrate that peace can provide more and better jobs than war.

One of the Economic Defence Council's missions is to develop European defence cooperation and encourage "spending efficiency". Why not apply the concept to reducing military expenditure throughout Europe, while inciting each EU member country to specialise in the areas where it is most successful? Instead of recruiting 35,000 new soldiers every year, we could recruit a third or half as many and use the remaining budget for youth skills-training projects in our disadvantaged neighbourhoods.

The other fields of power

Geopolitical power does not depend solely on military strength and Europe does not get the most out of its remarkable assets in other areas. Obviously if one takes into account only military might, the American empire reigns supreme. But on the basis of other indicators, Europe could very well be more powerful than the United States, if only it would make the political effort.

Without getting into an endless discussion about "soft power" à la Joseph Nye, we can look at components of power objectively from different angles. Notably, it is worth reviewing some of the figures, beginning with wealth indicators. In 2003, the European Union's GDP reached

$11,050 billion, for the first time higher than that of the United States, which came to a slightly lower $10,990 billion.[6] I have taken these figures and those that follow from the CIA's extremely useful *World Factbook*; I think we can safely assume that intelligence agencies need accurate knowledge of the world. The figures are all for 2003.

If we reason in terms of average wealth per capita, Americans are still ahead. Theoretically, the super-rich citizens of America have $37,800 each at their disposal but this figure conceals spectacular inequalities that cannot help but have negative effects on social cohesion and well-being. As a natural consequence of decades of neo-liberal policies, a tiny number of Americans, 0.1 per cent, or one in a thousand, now receive a 6 per cent share of national income. In 1978, this miniscule segment received "only" 2 per cent of national income. In less than thirty years, neo-liberal government policies have caused their share to triple. Just after the Second World War, the top 1 per cent of Americans were receiving 8 per cent of all national income; today they receive twice that. Inequalities have reached levels not seen since the 1920s.[7]

Theoretically, each European has $25,000 at his/her disposal, nearly $13,000 less than an American. As we have seen, however, averages are not helpful for understanding the real situation of a given population and for the moment at least, those $25,000 are better distributed, although inequalities are increasing steadily in Europe as well.

Another measure of wealth is national savings and reserves of gold and currency. By this criterion, Asia is the champion with $1,600 billion.[8] The United States has a miserable $86 billion nest egg whereas France and

Germany's combined reserves amount to $168 billion. In the event of a global stock market crash, you are better off in Asia, or failing that, in Europe.

The strength or weakness of a nation can also depend on its financial and commercial balances as well as the value and stability of its currency. Leading the list for the world's worst double deficit (both budget and trade) is, of course, the United States, with more than $2,000 billion worth of external debt (and at least $7,000 billion if you add the internal debt) – or 62 per cent of its GNP. France has no grounds for feeling superior with a public debt equal to 69 per cent of GNP.

Europe is more involved in, and dependent on global trade than the United States. Unlike the latter, it has a positive trade balance, still selling more than it buys abroad. Finally, in 2003, the United States attracted a slim 5 per cent of foreign investment flows worldwide, compared to 53 per cent going to Europe and 10 per cent to China. Here again, the EU is significantly more powerful than America.

The power of a region also depends on its industrial and agricultural stature. Among the top 100 transnational corporations, 41 are headquartered in euro-currency countries, 12 more in the United Kingdom and only 24 in the United States.[9] The task is to bring these giants under more effective financial and administrative control and remind them forcefully that they can't desert their native fiscal neighbourhood. They are becoming increasingly adept at tax avoidance using relocations, tax havens and "creative accounting".

On the agricultural side, the European Union exports at least 40 per cent of agricultural products commercialised worldwide, compared with a meagre 11 per cent from the United States. Europe has increased its harvested area and production by 50 per cent since the mid 1990s (this is for other reasons an extremely questionable policy but that is a different matter). The combined production of the United States and Europe accounts for 20 per cent of global agricultural production. Chinese production in contrast is running out of steam as its growing food imports attest – up 40 per cent between 2002 and 2003. This means China will be an increasingly good customer for Europe.

Europe's greatest weakness is, as noted, energy dependency – a worrying 80 per cent of its consumption; this is why the CED Report for 2005 expresses such concern. To become a true geostrategic power, Europe will have to ensure much greater energy self-sufficiency, using renewables, solar power and conservation as we shall see in the following chapter.

Another criterion for power is superiority in information and communications. The European Union and China both have more landlines and mobile phones than the United States. Although the US had a head start, Europe has also outpaced the US for the number and percentage of internet users with 34 per cent of all world internet users to the US's 20 per cent and China's 13 per cent. Since 2003, the EU–US gap has grown even more in Europe's favour.

Finally, let us not forget that a fairer, more just society is also a more powerful one. If Europe stops following the United States down the neo-liberal road to inequality and exclusion; if it comes together around a programme of peace-keeping, preservation and promotion of human and citizens' rights, social protection and public services, then we can watch as America exhausts itself in military spending and try not to feel too smug.[10]

Europe must aim for all these objectives. They are in the interests of every European citizen. We have the assets to become the new kind of geopolitical power the world needs, but the success of the project depends entirely on a particularly scarce resource: political will.

5

The Environmental Challenge

We know that we need an alternative Europe and we have excellent social, economic and political reasons for building it. We have also reviewed some of the great challenges Europeans will face in doing so. But what if life becomes virtually impossible from the sheer physical standpoint? If we devour our own substance, foul our nest and poison the earth, the sea and the air, what good is politics? We must place the environment at the very centre of the European project because if humans are to save their habitat, Europe is the only hope – this is the thesis I intend to defend.

One of the great mysteries of humankind's relationship with the natural systems on which it depends is this: we have all the ecological knowledge we need to act; it is available to all. Rarely has the scientific community reached such consensus on such a complex subject. The facts and the analysis are thoroughly established. The danger is not just to those "future generations" constantly invoked in political discourse but to our own. It is imminent; it is already happening; it is here and now.

The British government brought a number of climate experts to the "Stabilisation 2005" conference at Exeter in February 2005. They gave us at best ten years to change

course; beyond that the situation will become irreversible.*
Other experts forecast the disappearance of at least a million
living species by 2030, that is, tomorrow. Future disasters
in store for our own species are incommensurate with the
localised catastrophes we have seen so far, even those as
terrible and costly in human life as the tsunami of December
2004 and its quarter-million dead (or the floods in India,
Bangladesh and Britain in 2007).

The collapse of exhausted and vulnerable planetary
systems threatens not just personal health and safety, access
to food, water, medicine and the whole material basis of
our lives; but also strategic and geopolitical equilibrium,
social stability and world peace. This is why Al Gore fully
deserved the Nobel Peace Prize.

The facts

If you read at average speed, you have spent perhaps a couple
of hours up to now reading this book. As you were reading,
five or six living species died out and by the end of the day,
another 80 will have joined them. This year, we shall say
goodbye to about 30,000 species forever. In the 4 billion
years or so the planet has been whizzing around the Sun, it
has suffered five mass extinctions and each time, about 90
per cent of the organisms alive at the time were wiped out.

---

* For instance, the Siberian permafrost is melting. It contains
billions of tons of methane, a greenhouse gas 21 times as powerful
as CO_2. The area concerned is equivalent to the surface of France
and Germany: this means climate change will accelerate even
faster than previously thought. See www.newscientist.com/article/
mg18725124.500.html, and Ian Samples, *Guardian*, 11 August
2005.

You are undoubtedly familiar with the fifth great extinction – an asteroid slammed into the Yucatán Peninsula 65 million years ago, and bang! there went the dinosaurs. The catch is that we are right now in the midst of the sixth great extinction, and this time, we are the asteroid. Unfortunately for us, we are the dinosaurs as well...

You have probably heard also of "invasive species", those stowaways who gatecrash ecosystems that have no natural defences established to resist them. One of these invaders is the Nile perch. Someone tossed a couple into Lake Victoria a few decades ago where perch have proliferated, decimating some 200 species of fish once found there and ruining poor African fishermen. Or take the rabbits that constantly plague Australia or the brown tree snakes in Papua New Guinea which arrived literally by air, in the landing gear of small aircraft, and have since eaten most of the native bird species to extinction.

These are local disasters, but seen from the Earth's point of view, our own human species is a universal disaster. While estimates may vary, all the experts agree that human-induced extinction rates are at least a hundred-fold, perhaps a thousand-fold higher than the natural or "background" extinction rate.

Cod fishing off the Newfoundland coast yielded 300,000 tonnes in 1950, 800,000 tonnes in 1980 and zero tonnes in 2000. Is this a "local" phenomenon? Perhaps so, but research covering the totality of the world's seas reveals that in terms of weight, nine-tenths of the large fish species – tuna, swordfish, shark, and so on – have disappeared due to industrial trawlers.

This is an example of direct predation, but humans are also quite good at the indirect kind. They destroy the habitats of wild species by razing forests and eliminating habitats once rich in biodiversity. Savannahs are turned into grazing lands; intensive farming destroys hedgerows and uses massive chemical inputs. No room is left for birds, insects, small mammals, wild plants. The nitrogen contained in the 150 million tonnes of chemical fertilizers applied every year (compared to 14 million tonnes in 1950) is wiping out a huge number of aquatic and terrestrial species. If you eliminate too many species, you kill agriculture itself because chemistry cannot substitute for the services nature performs, given the chance, at no cost, like the renewal of soil fertility and pollination. Now alarming reports have appeared concerning the disappearance of bees and the literal collapse of their hives. Do we think we can pollinate our fruits and vegetables by hand?[1]

We now know that global warming accelerates and increases species decline and extinction. If temperatures rise too fast, natural habitat conditions change drastically. Plants and animals are unable to adapt or migrate quickly enough. The only ones that survive are those that can tolerate a broad range of conditions: nettles, flies, mosquitoes, crows… One major study dealing with the climate–species relationship in a variety of ecosystems came to the conclusion that, if present conditions remain unchanged, a fifth of all known species will disappear within thirty years and fully half in a hundred years.[2]

Since the early 1990s, the International Panel on Climate Change (IPCC), jointly founded in 1988 by the United Nations Environment Programme (UNEP), and the World Meteorological Organisation (WMO), has regularly published reports on global warming. The IPCC includes thousands of scientists from dozens of countries; its findings are widely known and broadly consensual in the scientific community. They are also extremely conservative because governments are able to intervene before any IPCC publication appears – which the United States, Saudi Arabia, China and other climate-change deniers regularly do. According to the IPCC, since the end of the nineteenth century, the global average surface temperature has increased by 0.6 °C; the predicted temperature increase over the next hundred years ranges between 1.5 and 4.5 °C. Many experts believe that out-of-control feedback effects could cause the thermometer to climb even more. Evidence of runaway feedback thrusts itself upon us daily, glaciers are receding faster than foreseen, the habitat of polar bears is disappearing. The United States and other governments insisted that all references to feedback mechanisms be deleted from the most recent IPCC reports. Such governments and a good part of the oil or motor vehicle industry are still trying to refute the IPCC's findings, but hundreds of scientists have been willing to put their reputations on the line in defending them.[3]

The Exeter "stability" conference of 2005 also lent its authority to predicting the dramatic consequences of global warming; these too have proven true and are accelerating. The Exeter scientists said forest fires would increase; that in Europe the areas around the Mediterranean will be hardest hit. In 2007, Olympia, birthplace of the Olympic games in 776 BC was attacked by the flames. Because biodiversity is in freefall, "half the world's population will live in regions where food crop losses will be significant"; these in turn will lead to migration on an enormous scale towards more favoured regions. In the United Kingdom, the government's chief scientific advisor informed Tony Blair that "global warming is a greater threat than terrorism".[4]

The United Nations is doing what it can to raise the alarm as well. One of its recent contributions is a broadly based study involving, like the IPCC, hundreds of scientists, 1,360 to be precise. Their research concerned a great variety of planetary ecosystems and the services these systems render to human beings. These physical ecosystems – mountain, polar, aquatic, urban, cultivated, savannah, coastal, river basin, woodland, arid, island and so on – were examined using a variety of criteria. Once more, the scientists involved were unanimous and arrived at the same conclusions as their colleagues from the IPCC and other organisations. They also introduced a conceptual dimension new to the UN – the notion of "natural capital" – which had not found its way into previous official reports.[5]

Most people concerned with ecological issues are familiar with the concept. During the 1980s and 1990s, the ecological economist Herman Daly unremittingly tried, and failed, to convince the World Bank to take natural capital into account. After more than a decade of frustrated efforts and tired of such a deaf and blind institution, Daly left the Bank and returned to academia. The ideas he tried to put across are nonetheless as simple as they are obvious.

To use the language of economics, nature represents a certain quantity of capital "stock". This stock is replenished, yes, but only at a certain rate which human beings have no power to speed up. We draw on this capital to satisfy our production requirements, but if the rate of withdrawal is faster than the rate of natural replenishment, we inevitably reduce the stock – this is a matter of simple arithmetic which anyone who has a bank account can understand. We can help nature to replenish the stock – for example by planting forests – but unfortunately humans undertake replenishment far less often than they destroy; they are better at deforestation and other kinds of irresponsible destruction. So-called "traditional" farmers have always worked with the notion of natural capital even though they would never use the term. They let the soil rest, rotate their crops, use compost and few or no chemicals and so on – partly because they are poor. Modern agriculture is in a hurry, which is why in the American Mid-Western bread basket, at least five metres of topsoil have already disappeared.

The accounting methods of capitalist societies are in this regard worse than useless. They are utterly incapable of telling us what we urgently need to know; their techniques are not merely primitive but dangerous. Not only do our accounts not supply us with necessary information; they lull us into thinking we are far richer than we actually are. If a company listed on the stock exchange spent down its capital the way we spend our natural capital, it would soon go bankrupt. Capitalism's ecological short-sightedness has reached truly criminal proportions.*

The United Nations report *Millennium Ecosystem Assessment* should be credited with a breakthrough because it enumerates the "services rendered to human beings" by various ecosystems and measures their capacity to continue providing these services. Of the 24 ecosystem types studied by the UN teams, only four have increased their capacity to provide services. For example, the yield from cultivated land was multiplied by 2.5 between 1960 and 2000, although this was chiefly due to the increase in harvested area. Fish and shellfish farming in coastal waters is an expanding industry,

---

* I can only touch on these topics here. For a somewhat more adequate treatment, see Susan George, *Another World is Possible If...* (Verso, 2004), chapter 2.

especially in Asia, but this has given rise to other problems – dramatically demonstrated when the tsunami struck. One reason the tidal wave was so devastating can be traced to the destruction of mangrove swamps, replaced by vast shrimp-farming ponds. The lush and tangled mangroves are no longer there to provide protection against such disasters.

The UN scientific teams identified five other ecosystems considered stable in some parts of the world but declining in others. The service-providing capacity of 15 ecosystems out of the 24 studied was in overall decline, most alarmingly for the provision of fish, firewood, fresh water and wild and medicinal plants.

We are spending down our natural capital with abandon, but on the books it looks positive because this destruction contributes to "economic growth". The example Herman Daly chose twenty years ago is no less pertinent today – who cares how many saw-mills or industrial fishing boats you own if there are no fish and no trees left?

Capitalist arithmetic has another serious flaw: it cannot predict the future because it fails to recognise feedback effects, critical thresholds or "tipping points". An extra tonne of CO_2 let loose in the atmosphere; another species gone forever will register, if it registers at all, as just another unit added to one side of the scales. This arithmetic says $1 + 1 + 1 = 3$, but at some unpredictable point an addition can equal infinity, because at a given threshold the whole system will undergo radical change and collapse – and we have no idea when that threshold may be crossed. Thus we cannot fully predict the future impacts of global warming because the feedbacks may either cancel each other out or reinforce each other (such processes are called "feedback loops"). Because mathematical proof positive is unattainable, our "decision-makers" avoid making any decisions at all, or such trivial ones that they have no real impact on the state of the environment.

Despite the wealth of research, repeated conferences and recurrent warnings, officialdom is asleep, paralysed or impotent. Because they are heavily influenced by industrial lobbies, the implicit governmental response is "None of the dangers you point to can actually happen and the proof is that they haven't happened yet." As *New Scientist* pointed out after the Exeter "Stabilisation 2005" conference, "It is as if the politicians are still operating in a parallel universe where natural laws do not apply. They would never dare to deal with fiscal meltdown in the same cavalier manner."[6]

The hollow and ritualistic phrase "sustainable development" means absolutely nothing in the case of 95 per cent of the people who use it but has served to gain time for "free and undistorted competition" and allowed the all-powerful market to reign for a few extra decades. Humanity pretends it is alone on Earth – the "master and possessor of nature". Marxism is if anything worse in this department. We are bogged down in nineteenth-century ideologies and accounting systems and consequently we have adopted an ostrich policy, completely incapable of forging relevant tools for building a new model. The capitalist system in its entirety – as well as Chinese "socialism" – stands in the way of acknowledging ecological reality.

The excellence of apes

Self-importance, pretentiousness, the apparent human inability to face facts reminds me of the words of Heraclitus, the pre-Socratic Greek philosopher:

To a god the wisdom of the wisest man sounds apish. Beauty in a human face looks apish too. In everything we have attained the excellence of apes.[7]

Twenty-five hundred years later, we have barely evolved. For once, we should attempt to use reason and rise above the level of primates.

What can a Greek philosopher of 500 BC possibly have to do with Europe and, specifically, with the Constitution or the new Treaty? The Constitution is typically simian where the environment is concerned (as elsewhere). In the Constitution, the environment was present in Parts I, II and III. The text says:

> The Union shall work for the sustainable development of Europe based on balanced economic growth and price stability, a highly competitive social market economy, aiming at full employment and social progress, and a high level of protection and improvement of the quality of the environment. (I-3, 3)

"Sustainable development" is therefore based on economic growth and our old friend, the "highly-competitive social market economy", which immediately disqualifies it for any claims to ecological improvements. Returning to the preceding paragraph of the same article concerning the objectives of the Union, we are reminded that the Union intends to "offer [...] an internal market where competition is free and undistorted".

Competition, however, could also be "distorted" if the Commission finds that environmental standards are "too high". Do you want to rid your roads of super-polluting trucks and your tables of pesticide-drenched strawberries? Good luck. The WTO has repeatedly ruled on disputes with an ecological aspect, and every time it has ruled that environmental protection measures were in fact "disguised barriers to trade". There is no reason to believe Europe would behave any differently – and the texts provide all the tools it needs.

The phrase "price stability" in the same article is an allusion to the "stability pact" and to the independence of the Central Bank, whose only mission is to guarantee the said stability. The TEC, rejected by the French and Dutch, made it impossible to issue bonds (that is, borrow) in order to make substantial investments in environmental protection.

The environment briefly returns in Part II devoted to the Charter of Fundamental Rights:

A high level of environmental protection and the improvement of the quality of the environment must be integrated into the policies of the Union and ensured in accordance with the principle of sustainable development. (II-97)

This may sound great, but aside from the fact that the Charter itself is devoid of any legal value and creates "no new competences or extension of the Union's powers", it does not define "sustainable development" either, so we are stuck with the definition in Part I. And thus we come full circle, because sustainable development is subservient to economic growth and to the market. Any remaining hope that this "high level of environmental protection" could be incorporated into the Union's policies is stopped dead once we get down to serious matters in Part III where the Charter is unceremoniously seen off.

Two long articles, III-233 and 234, deal with the environment. The first thing we learn is that no environmental taxes may be introduced without the unanimous consent of the Member States. So much for taxes on CO_2 or on aircraft fuel. Unanimity is also required for measures concerning the "development of [the Union's] regions" or the "management of water resources", and those which could affect "a Member State's choice between different energy sources".

Readers who neglect to refer to Article III-172 (which itself refers to Article III-130), as Article III-233 tells them to do, will miss certain crucial points. All the environmental measures the Commission adopts must be in conformity with the four great freedoms of movement (goods, services, capital, people), as demanded by III-130. The provisions in III-172 are even better: the Commission must adopt "harmonisation measures" for national environmental provisions. Here the penny drops: we can only be talking about harmonisation downwards, towards the lowering of protection and standards because if a Member State intends to "maintain national provisions [...] relating to the protection of the environment" or to introduce new ones "based on new scientific evidence", it must "notify the Commission of these provisions as well as the grounds for maintaining them".

The all-powerful Commission will then decide whether these measures represent an "arbitrary discrimination or a disguised restriction on trade between Member States and whether or not they constitute an obstacle to the functioning of the internal market". Again, it is the Commission which

We the Peoples of Europe

"adopts a European decision approving or rejecting the national provisions". In other words, it is exactly the same disaster scenario we know from the WTO.

Thanks to Robert Joumard's remarkable concordance between Constitution and Reform Treaty, I can confidently say that all these articles remain intact somewhere in the new Treaty: the only change is the addition of a reference to combating climate change in what was Article 233. We have few reasons for optimism for the planet's future as seen by Europe.

Civilisations are mortal

In his book *Collapse*, Professor Jared Diamond of UCLA, examines the reasons for the collapse and disappearance of a number of past societies.[8]

Diamond, who describes himself as a "bio-geographer-evolutionist-psychologist", identifies several factors determining the success or failure of a society: the inherent fragility of the society's physical environment, climate stability, its relations – friendly or hostile – with neighbours and trading partners, and most important of all, "how the society solves its ecological problems". Diamond's case studies, from the Mayan empire to Easter Island, have several things in common including the overexploitation of resources which leads, imperceptibly at first, to social dissolution, a point of no return and social breakdown. Another common characteristic is a powerful elite in a position to keep on consuming long after resource scarcity has hit the less well-off. The elite has the means to live in a fool's paradise, cut off from the rest of society. Does this remind you of anything?

Assuming we would rather not end up this way ourselves, we have to act fast and decisively. We cannot be content with a couple of lacklustre paragraphs putting the Commission in charge of our destiny and leaving the market in charge. Progressives must place the environment at the heart of the European project and the next stages of its development. In the name of a responsible Europe, we must review critically the letter and the spirit of present European environmental provisions. Such an approach is in the interests of every individual Member State, of Europe collectively and of the world as a whole.

Politically and culturally, Europe has a huge responsibility because neither the United States nor China will undertake such a programme and the developing countries cannot yet afford to do so. That leaves Europe and it is up to Europeans to show that change is possible.

First, we need an honest ecological assessment and we must force politicians to accept it: Europe is living beyond its ecological means. Like the elites of fallen empires, Europeans continue to consume more than their share by drawing excessively on the natural capital of others. The difference is that unlike the elite of Easter Island or the Mayas, they do it globally. The means available to a society, assuming it relies on its own resources, can be measured objectively and uniformly across societies thanks to the concept of the "ecological footprint". This measurement, devised by Professor William Rees of the University of British Columbia in Vancouver, allows us to gauge the impact of a given population on nature and the capacity of that population's own resources to support a lifestyle determined by income. Nature not only has to withstand ever-increasing human numbers, but also a far "heavier" humanity, because the wealthy consume so much more than the poor. The ecological footprint is defined as

> The corresponding area of productive land and aquatic ecosystems required to produce the resources used, and to assimilate the wastes produced, by a given population at a specified material standard of living, wherever on Earth that land may be located.[9]

Thanks to the footprint method which conflates population and affluence, we can observe, for example, that feeding London requires the entire productive land area of the United Kingdom; or that the Netherlands requires between five and seven times its actual landmass, and so on.

Second, we need enough humility to acknowledge that human systems are embedded in nature, not vice versa. We have to adapt to nature because, beyond a certain point, nature will no longer be able to adapt to us. Humans are naturally anthropocentric; nothing is more important for us than our own species with its myriad economic, social and political arrangements – but from nature's standpoint, humans are like cancer. Natural systems would be objectively much better off without us and life as a whole would be far more abundant if our species disappeared and left the space we have colonised to others.

It remains to be seen whether we can for once surpass the excellence of apes and devise policies for a Europe for the common good guided by ecological principles.

How should we go about it? Well-meaning advice abounds in ecological handbooks and the popular press urging "us" to change our personal habits in order to save life on earth and to move towards "de-growth" or *la décroissance* as

French environmentalists call it. A quick browse on the internet yields the following nuggets of advice: get rid of your television so you will be less tempted to consume and become more creative; free yourself from your car which not only emits greenhouse gasses but causes accidents and oil wars; refuse to travel by aeroplane; reject mobile phones and, while you're at it, the microwave oven, the lawnmower and other useless products of consumer society; boycott suburban malls and supermarkets which go hand in hand with the automobile and kill off small businesses and favour large-scale, capital-intensive agriculture; eat less meat, or better still no meat at all; don't drink bottled water and consume only local products rather than those transported over vast distances and finally, that perennial favourite, change your lightbulbs.

In other words, change your behaviour and your lightbulbs and the world will change. Hmmmm. Let's assume for a moment that 10–20 per cent of Europeans take this advice to heart and apply it starting tomorrow morning – a wild hypothesis to begin with – such a change in lifestyles would barely scratch the surface and would certainly not touch the underlying problems. Let me be clear: I do not want to discourage individual efforts, often the first step towards common action, and I admire people whose lifestyles are in harmony with their ecological principles. But let's face it: not only is it virtually impossible to follow these recommendations and continue to lead a "normal" life; it is much more important to fight for national and European environmental policies that address root causes and our predatory relationship to the environment. If we don't introduce such policies voluntarily today, we will be forced to do so under duress tomorrow. And when people finally understand they are in immediate ecological peril, it might be easier for some totalitarian force to use popular anxiety to its own advantage, just as George Bush used fear of terrorism to wage war abroad and threaten the fundamental freedoms of Americans at home.

If even widespread individual awareness is not enough, what political power could lead an ecological revolution? We can attempt an answer by process of elimination.

The United States? The very suggestion is a cruel joke when we know that the US has not even ratified the Kyoto Protocol, itself a meek and mild instrument. One hundred and eighty-two States have approved the Convention on Biological Diversity which emerged from the 1992 Rio Conference, but not the United States.

In their own backyard they gave the go-ahead to cut down the last virgin forests to facilitate oil-drilling, even in national parks. In July 2005 at the G-8 meeting, when George Bush reluctantly admitted that global warming was partly due to human activity, everyone applauded as if the world had just taken a giant step forward. Alas, no. The current American president is still adamant that reduction of CO_2 emissions is contrary to US economic interests and any future one is likely to lend a dutiful ear to the same old lobbies that have colluded with the climate devil before.

Capitalist greed does not, however, fully explain American indifference to environmental destruction. Another cause, virtually inconceivable for Europeans, is Christian evangelical fundamentalism – a movement followed by at least 70 million people. Not all of them, thank God, are indifferent to the environment, but these Americans believe in the literal truth of the Bible, particularly the Book of Genesis in which God gave Man dominion over the earth and all its creatures to use – or such is their interpretation – as he sees fit.* They also believe that the Apocalypse is nigh, that Christ will return and that true believers will go straight to heaven before the final destruction of sinners and the world – a horrendous vision they will be spared (or perhaps enjoy watching from their heavenly front row seats).†

Their doctrine can be summarised in few words: the world cannot be saved. Aside from attending to his or her own personal salvation, the believer has no obligations to the Earth and precious few towards fellow humans. As one commentator observed, why worry about the Earth when drought, floods, famine and other environmental disasters to come are signs of the much-awaited Apocalypse? Why bother about global warming when your own place in heaven is secure?

Aside from the Christian fundamentalists, there are plenty of Americans who don't believe the Bible is the literal truth but who simply want to keep driving their SUVs and heating their houses to 23 °C. We can count on these 4 per cent of the world's population to continue to contribute a quarter of total world CO_2 emissions.

---

* See Bill Moyers, "Welcome to Doomsday", *The New York Review of Books*, 24 March 2005. A poll published in *Newsweek* showed that 36 per cent of respondents believed that the Book of Revelations (Apocalypse) is literally true prophecy; another published in *Time Magazine* revealed that a quarter of the American population believed the Bible predicted the 9/11 attacks. This would indicate that somewhere between 70 to 100 million Americans are fundamentalist believers.

† To find out how much time you have before being incinerated in the final conflagration, ask your search engine to look for "rapture index". See also my book, *Hijacking America: How the Religious and Secular Right Changed What Americans Think* (Polity, 2008).

So what is the outlook for an environmental crusade led by China or India? I can hear you laughing. China will probably soon manufacture ecologically friendly products like solar panels just as it produces toys or underwear, but this production is unlikely to have much impact on the country's own environmental practices. The Chinese and the Indians (and doubtless even more the first than the second) seem determined to repeat the same awful mistakes we made in the West during the nineteenth and twentieth centuries. Hence their fascination for huge, "pharaonic" development projects like dams which uproot millions of poor people and contribute to environmental destruction. The Chinese want to drive private automobiles and we in the West are not exactly well placed to say they shouldn't have them. Even well-educated Chinese living in Beijing, where one rarely catches a glimpse of blue sky, actually believe you can acquire immunity from pollution. In both India and China, the World Bank is still financing highly polluting low-grade coal-fired power plants.

Who can believe that the United States, China or India can provide the planet with the slightest ecological hope as they nonchalantly continue down the road that ends in a brick wall. The only faint hope lies with us and for this reason the European project must be ecological.

Sceptics might welcome such a project more readily if we can show them that it is not just technically feasible but economically profitable. Leading-edge environmental technologies will play a large future role and will be much in demand. Countries capable of providing them, as several European countries are already doing, will reap major economic benefits. Spanish and Danish wind turbine manufacturers and German alternative energy technologies are today enjoying spectacular commercial success.

We would do well to use the funds allocated to the Common Agricultural Policy not to subsidise capital-intensive agricultural producers but to help those practising eco-agriculture, replanting hedgerows and leaving strips of uncultivated land between fields for wild species. We could provide subsidies for the conversion to organic farming while levying a tax on chemical fertilizers and pesticides. We could help communities forge links with co-operatives of local producers, encouraging them to favour food producers close to home.

Europe should pressure its transnational corporations to reduce their CO_2 emissions. For example BP, the largest UK company, emitted 85 million tonnes of CO_2 in 2004 compared with 83 million in 2003. It spilled an estimated 5.7 million litres of oil into the sea in 2004.[10] These figures are published; they are in the public domain, and the mere fact that we can know them means that we could also tax them.

Do we really want to remain dependent on oil that costs over $90 a barrel, as it did in November 2007? On a fuel that comes mainly from the most unstable region on earth, pollutes our cities and poisons our seas? If so, then we need only continue as we are. If not, then we must urgently develop alternatives for an industrial society: we can't go back to some mythical, idealised rural paradise. Prototypes have already proven that using much lighter materials (carbon fibres in particular) in the automotive or aviation industries, we could reduce fuel consumption by at least two-thirds. These materials are also more resistant, safer in the event of collision, as well as cheaper and easier to shape and assemble, but they remain expensive because they are not yet mass-produced.

Until we can make a full transition to a hydrogen economy, we can develop other sources of energy. So called bio-fuels are not the answer however, except locally and in particular circumstances where they do not steal land from food crops and from small producers.* The US's quick transition to agro-fuels has been a boon to the largest farmers by doubling wheat prices and pushing up other grain prices as well, but they are also fast becoming what George Monbiot has called an "agricultural crime against humanity".[11] Brazil has exported sugar-cane based ethanol for years, now with particular success to China and Japan. But if Europe adopts the same solution as it shows every sign of doing, we may well become complicit in that crime. Better to concentrate on energy savings (especially in the construction and automotive industries) and on the sources provided for free by sun, wind, water and waves. Public spending will be needed because private companies generally refuse to go first into uncharted territory. The cost of developing an efficient carbon fibre industry in the United States has been estimated at $90 billion but would require government investment. In Europe, the figures would range between €60 billion and €70 billion. Such investments would pay off rapidly and handsomely, thanks to cost-reduction and the elimination of what economists call "externalities" – pollution, health problems, accidents and so on. If we

* Poor countries that have neglected their food sovereignty for years will have to import far more expensive food and, as always, the poor will suffer first. Bio-fuels made from non-food crops or those grown on heretofore unproductive land are another story and should be explored even though they too may endanger smallholders.

had a European Central Bank that behaved like a normal central bank, it would be easy to find enough money for such investments, but unfortunately it is extremely difficult with the one we have now.*

Governments should introduce "eco-friendly" building standards and enforce increasingly stringent rules to promote energy-efficient homes, offices, shops and so on. Other industrial innovations should concern the use of particular metals, different CO_2 absorbing paints, green roofs, lighter materials, improved motors etc. Here again, the prototypes exist, the technical measures needed have already been devised. Furthermore, an ecological society is the greatest reservoir of jobs ever invented, with a huge potential for eradicating unemployment. Technical change does not exclude behavioural change – Europeans should still act in an eco-friendly way and be profoundly embarrassed at the sight of, say, a woman weighing 50 kilos driving around in an SUV that weighs 5,000.

Concern for the environment can no longer be seen as secondary in the European future. It must guide our daily lives, our everyday acts, our politics and our governments. Nothing is more urgent.

---

* The ECB found €350 billion easily enough when European banks that had stupidly invested in subprime mortgage-related securities came to its door, caps in hand.

6
Social Insecurity

Unemployment, lack of job security, escalating inequalities, privatisation, threatened public services, relocation, all-out liberalisation and social regression: the European situation today, for most of us, is not encouraging. Neo-liberals, however, want it that way because however bad these phenomena may be for working people, they do encourage the accumulation of capital, keep a "flexible" workforce ready to serve under unfavourable conditions and help the rich get richer. I have tried to show throughout this book that these goals underlie the Constitution and that they have an impact on every European citizen.

The question now is how to restore individual and collective security and guarantee it for the future. What are its components and how can we make sure that all Europeans have a right to "the pursuit of happiness" which the American Declaration of Independence called an "inalienable right", as important as the rights to life and liberty.

No institution to my knowledge has better defined human security in the context of neo-liberal globalisation than the International Labour Organisation (ILO) in a comprehensive and extremely well-documented study. Here I shall do it the injustice of summarising it.[1]

For several years, the ILO has placed the notion of "decent work" at the centre of its concerns and the aim of the study called *Economic Security for a Better World* is to enrich this concept. It examines the complexity of the notion of "work" and identifies the entire range of components that contribute to economic security which, taken together, go a good way towards guaranteeing human fulfilment.

The ILO team begin by acknowledging that insecurity has increased for the great majority of the world's population and they undertake a sharp, well-founded critique of neo-liberal globalisation, the Washington Consensus, the international financial institutions, the World Trade Organisation and financial markets – criticism any self-respecting opponent of neo-liberalism should welcome. Unlike most of these opponents, however, the ILO enjoys the advantages of a large staff of full-time professionals, high-level consultants, "dozens of statisticians and researchers in the social sciences", not to mention the means to carry out its own surveys independently. In the present case, the researchers questioned 48,000 interviewees and visited 10,000 companies over a period of four years in order to produce this report. The result is an unequalled database covering a hundred countries. Ninety of them, home to 85 per cent of the world's population, are then classified according to various indexes of economic security. This monumental piece of work deserves to be better known; it is a kind of classic like the annual Human Development Reports of the United Nations Development Programme (UNDP), except that the ILO *magnum opus* looks like being a one-off.

Here is the gist of what it covers. First, at the macro-economic level, peoples' economic security is measurably deteriorating. This is a global phenomenon, whether the causes are natural, economic, financial or social disasters. For example, in the Latin America–Caribbean region alone, between 1980 and 1998, over forty economic and financial crises took place in which the GNP per capita plunged by more than 4 per cent. More than ninety countries – from Algeria to Zimbabwe – experienced at least one "severe" monetary crisis between 1990 and 2001. How bad is "severe"? The ILO's definition is a crisis in which the value of the currency drops by at least 25 per cent in a single month; that this drop is at least 10 per cent higher than the drop of the previous month. Twenty-five per cent the second month and at least 15 per cent the first means we are talking about a two-month plunge of 40 per cent at minimum. Concretely, peoples' savings, pensions, salaries, incomes are savaged.[2]

"Natural" disasters, especially those related to climate change, affected 600 million people in 2002 – three times as many as in an average year during the 1990s. I do not have figures for subsequent years but doubtless 2004, the year of the tsunami, was another record-breaker. Apart from India and China, neither of which has implemented full-blown neo-liberal policies, economic growth since 1980 has been distinctly less vigorous than during the period 1960–80 when the average annual growth rate reached 4.6 per cent. Since 1980, it has been only 2.6 per cent.

Privatisation has proven expensive financially and damaging socially. The ILO notes that:

it is ironic that at the same time as privatisation is being extended to social policy on a large scale [...] there is growing evidence of its high costs and deficiencies in providing adequate social protection. [For example], the switch to a private pension system has cost the Chilean government about 5 per cent of GNP during the last 20 years – much more than it would have cost to eradicate poverty altogether.

The Argentine mega-financial crisis was also fuelled by "the public expenditure needed to finance the switch of the pension fund from a public to a Chilean-style private system", a demand of the IMF, one among many damaging policies. But the Chicago Boys and the Washington Consensus Mandarins got their way, and that, after all, is what counts.

In Mexico, after the North American Free Trade Agreement (NAFTA) entered into force, the total number of jobs may have increased but real wages dropped to levels lower than they were twenty years previously, despite increases in productivity. Nor did anyone foresee that after 2002, hundreds of thousands of Mexican manufacturing jobs in hundreds of "maquiladora" factories along the US border would migrate to China.

Southern countries are increasingly dependent on remittances sent home by their emigrants – in the case of Pakistan, the Philippines, Mexico, and several Central American countries, the "exported labourer" is the nation's most lucrative export. According to the United Nations, migrants' remittances amount officially to $200 billion; unofficially the totals are much higher. Even the conservative figure is more than double the money provided by official development aid. According to the ILO, the flow of people is just as massive. It counts 175 million emigrant workers (3 per cent of world population and twice as many as in 1980); 10 million official refugees; 20–25 million people displaced inside their own countries (an especially severe phenomenon in Africa) and about a million victims of people-trafficking; a growth industry worth at least $12 billion a year according to the United States government.

Neo-liberal globalisation has significantly increased the rights of capital, just as the capacity of States to regulate monetary flows and those of workers to move freely have steadily shrunk. Labour exporting countries are losing their young men and women (who work abroad as maids, nannies and sometimes prostitutes); so they lose their most dynamic and best educated people. Northern governments use increasingly harsh methods to deal with immigrants, including detention camps and physical restraints.

The seven pillars of security

Such is the bleak worldwide tableau for individual and collective economic security. With regard to work, the ILO ranks countries according to their performance in seven slightly overlapping but not identical security categories. European countries invariably figure at the top of these categories; this is why I find the ILO's work valuable in illustrating the reality of the European model. It undeniably exists and deserves to be protected and preserved. Here is a brief definition of each category:

Income security. The ILO defines income security in terms of adequacy, continuity and fairness. It is "an adequate level of income, a reasonable assurance that such an income will continue, a sense that the income is fair relative to actual and perceived 'needs' and relative to the income of others; and the assurance of compensation or support in the event of a shock or crisis affecting income" beyond the individual's control.

This concept is especially rich because it includes salaries and social benefits such as paid holidays, in-family transfers, free or employer-subsidised meals, subsidised transport, health insurance and "public goods", from which "public ills" are subtracted, such as living in a dangerous neighbourhood or a polluted area. "Needs" also influence the measurement – for example, the United States is "richer" than Europe in terms of revenue per capita, but the sense of personal insecurity means Americans spend hundreds of millions of dollars yearly on arms, anti-theft measures, safe rooms and the like just as they must invariably spend on private transport.

Europe's relatively high income security is under attack from all sides; its adversaries use different weapons. One little-known instrument is wielded by private credit-rating agencies which strongly influence the financial markets. These agencies put pressure on individual European governments and threaten to trigger a rise in interest rates if the government refuses to reduce its social spending, especially on health care. This is politically explosive in Europe, a continent of aging populations. The rating agencies also demand higher defence budgets. The government that disregards this "advice" may find that its bonds are no longer rated triple AAA but have slipped to AA or B grade, thus forcing the government to pay bondholders higher interest rates because of the supposed "additional risk" which is in fact non-existent. The major bondholders like pension funds and other institutional investors are not interested in the government's side of the argument; they want their "risk premium". This is one further example of the extent of financial market influence on State decisions.

The rankings in this first category show Finland – generally among the highest ranking countries in the various categories of economic security, coming in behind not just other countries of "old Europe" but even behind newcomers like the Czech Republic, Latvia, Poland and Slovakia.

Labour market security. This category reflects supply – the number of jobs on offer – and demand – the number of workers who want them. Security means ample employment opportunities in good conditions; insecurity means that workers stay in their jobs and do not make demands on the employer for fear of losing their jobs and not finding new ones. If unemployed, they must take more or less what they can get. From the capitalist point of view, labour market insecurity provides excellent discipline.

The extent of this type of security is measured by (1) the participation rate of each age bracket in the economically active population and (2) the overall unemployment rate and average duration of unemployment. The longer the period of average unemployment, the lower the labour market security. France has one of the lowest proportions in the world of people over 50 in the economically active population; but this kind of insecurity is increasing everywhere. In the EU-15, about 8 per cent of potential workers are unemployed, but the rate is far worse in the newly acceded Central European countries and worse still for foreign-born workers, the young and the old. This measurement does not take into account the numbers of people stuck in involuntary part-time work, a particular problem for large numbers of women. None of the Central countries rank high in this category, and Luxembourg obtains a lower score than other countries of the EU-15.

Employment security. This category takes in the protection of the salaried or waged worker against job loss, arbitrary dismissal and his or her right to compensation if unjustly dismissed. It is measured by the probability of keeping one's job and the legal protection granted to those who are employed. Obviously, people in casual, precarious or temporary work have zero security in this regard and this is also the case for the vast majority of the world's workers.

The IMF and the Organisation of Economic Cooperation and Development (OECD), the club of the richest countries, ritually denounce employment security, claiming that it leads to artificially high unemployment rates.* Someone seems to be listening. Surveys in industrialised countries indicate that an increasing proportion of employees answer "Yes" to the question: "Do you think you will lose your present job during the next twelve months?" Other studies show, unsurprisingly, that this anxiety about losing one's job has a strong impact on employees' physical and mental health.

The decline of the public and manufacturing sectors, both of which provide relatively stable employment, and the concomitant rise in the proportion of service industry jobs accentuates this trend. In the 1990s, the Economic Security

* This is a leitmotif at the OECD: see its annual *Employment Outlook*, various years.

We the Peoples of Europe

Index declined in 16 of 21 industrialised countries where the ILO was able to measure it.

In this category, the EU-15 countries remain well ahead of the others, except for the United Kingdom. The United States, Japan, Australia and Canada also lag far behind.

Work security defines protection against physical, mental and psychological hazards in the workplace. This concept goes beyond the traditional notion of "workplace health and safety" because it includes more modern hazards like stress, overwork and a new category the ILO calls "presenteeism", as opposed to absenteeism, as well as moral and sexual harassment. According to this organisation, at least two million people die each year from work-related diseases and accidents, and this figure is soaring.

During the twentieth century, developed countries adopted workplace security codes, signed international conventions, established work inspection agencies and encouraged companies to create security departments and committees. Neo-liberals everywhere are trying to abolish a good many of these measures and replace them with what they call the "individual responsibility model", "self-regulation", or purely market regulation. They claim that regulations impose too heavy a cost burden on companies and force them to seek out casual or illegal workers as replacements when sickness and accident benefits for permanent contract workers are too expensive.

In this category, Central European countries (except for Slovenia), Austria, Greece, Ireland, and the United Kingdom have comparatively low ratings.

Skills security involves acquiring and maintaining levels of proficiency and training. It can be measured by the availability of training opportunities, continuing education and apprenticeships, starting with basic education in the country's school system. Skill security allows workers to develop their abilities and to work in socially and economically useful professions. The ILO, UNESCO, which publishes an annual report on "Education for All", and the United Nations in its "Millennium Goals", have coined the phrase "educational poverty line". The great majority of the world's workers fall below this line. The concept of skills security is comparable to what corporations call "human capital".

By undermining educational systems throughout the South, the World Bank has contributed disproportionately to the decline of skills security. Its structural adjustment programmes emphasise "cost recovery" (i.e. fee-paying) in education; their effect is to limit the numbers of pupils and the number of years they stay in school. These programmes also reduce the economic security of teachers whose salaries may be sharply cut or even disappear altogether. The OECD has also pushed the "market-oriented approach" to education, in which the "supply" of education is calculated to correspond to the "demand" of the labour market. Even UNESCO now cheerleads for the World Bank in making education a marketable commodity whose success is measured by "rates of return". One of the many trade agreements under the umbrella of the World Trade Organisation, the GATS or General Agreement on Trade in Services, lists education as one of twelve commercial service sectors. The trend is overwhelmingly towards standardisation, often called "Americanisation", of education and in many cases transnational corporations are the providers of professional training.

Many Central European countries have reached EU-15 standards in this category. Among the 15 themselves, only Austria and Italy lag behind.

Job security concerns the extent of the worker's capacity to determine and control his or her job description and the possibilities for building a career. Many employees enjoy "employment security", meaning they are relatively safe from redundancies, but are forced to "adapt", which implies they are subject to unwelcome change, which can be stressful. On the other hand, the absence of any change can be as bad or worse. Holding the same job throughout your working life, whether on an assembly line or as a supermarket cashier, provides minimum personal fulfilment and job satisfaction. In Southern countries, one rarely finds scope for "career development" and other future-oriented pursuits – the challenge is to survive in the present. For the ILO, however, "decent work" means career opportunities, not just having a job.

The measurement of this security is subjective because it is related to personal satisfaction. Among the EU-15, the lowest ranking countries are Greece, Ireland, Italy and the United Kingdom (plus Switzerland).

Security of representation implies "having a voice" – being able to defend your rights and interests – but also, a more profound sense to determine your identity as a human being. This involves the capacity to negotiate, to become informed and to evaluate social and employment policies. The "voice" is both individual and collective. The individual must gain access to institutions and the processes which guarantee rights. Workers collectively must have access to an independent and competent union that can negotiate in their name. The ILO's basic conventions aim to guarantee the right of association, the right to organise, to join a trade union and to bargain collectively.

With the spread of globalisation, this "voice" has weakened, and has sometimes gone totally silent. The framework for social and economic rights is increasingly focused on American law – using litigation rather than regulation. Everywhere in the world, trade union movements have encountered setbacks.

All Western European countries rank well in this category, unlike the newer EU members.

The security index

From these seven categories of economic security, the ILO derives an index or country-ranking system through a complex process of weighing and comparing the different kinds of security. The result is a classification of countries in four categories, carefully named so as not to offend. The ILO believes that this index is at least a roughly objective guide to levels of contentment, individual well-being and social cohesion, at least in so far as they are determined by everyday economic activity.

Europe is clearly at the forefront of this world index. In the group of best-performing countries, called the "pace-setters", 17 are Western and four are Central European. The other top countries are Canada, Japan and Israel. Although a social model can always be improved, the ILO finds the worker and citizen protection policies in these countries are "exemplary". The Scandinavian countries occupy the top slots, probably because of their high level of union membership.

Next on the scale come the countries in the "pragmatists" group – they include the United States, Australia, New Zealand, South Korea, South Africa and Chile. The United States has refused to ratify any of the basic ILO conventions and makes no legal provision for payments in cases of mass layoffs. The US deliberately makes the task of trade unions more difficult, often through costly and prolonged litigation.

Further down the scale, the euphemisms come thick and fast. The third group of "conventional" countries includes Brazil, Argentina, Russia and most of the former socialist republics that have obvious "governance" problems. Rock bottom are all the others, the vast majority in the "much to be done" category, including the demographic heavyweights like India, China, Pakistan, Bangladesh, all of Africa, as well as Mexico and most of the Middle East.*

As for Europe, the first EU countries, the Six, then the Twelve and finally the Fifteen are always at the top of the scale, a fact which by itself should convince sceptics that the "European model" indeed exists, that it is mathematically quantifiable and that its outcomes are ethically superior to those in other countries. It is objective proof of a collective

---

* The composite ILO index for the seven kinds of security or Economic Security Index (ESI) is as follows for the top 25 countries: Sweden (0.977), Finland, Norway, Denmark, Netherlands, Belgium, France, Luxembourg, Germany, Canada, Ireland, Austria, Spain, Portugal, United Kingdom, Switzerland, Australia, Japan, Israel, Italy, Hungary, Slovakia, Czech Republic, New Zealand, United States (0.612).

social achievement, largely due, as we know, to popular struggles over decades. This said, the next observation is that the European model is everywhere under threat. Under the protective cover of globalisation, national and international elites are clearly out to destroy it. The president of the MEDEF (Movement of French Enterprises), Madame Laurence Parisot, put it frankly. As soon as she took office, she declared, "Freedom of thought ends where the Labour Code begins."

Gérard Filoche, a work inspector and Socialist who campaigned for the "No", commented:

> This says it all: anything that protects the weak or is based on republican legality; anything that stands for the lawful State inside a corporation, curbs the exploitation of workers and organises trade union rights, collective bargaining agreements, representative bodies for personnel, reduces workplace accidents and work-related illness; anything that limits casual labour, imposes a minimum wage; provides professional training, penalises widespread employer delinquency; maintains a modicum of human dignity in periods of unemployment; places ceilings on working hours, supplies industrial medicine – all this is in the Labour Code, the result of decades of social struggles; and now Madame Parisot, who finds all this prohibits "freedom of thought", is head of the MEDEF.[3]

The elite's project to reduce economic security requires that it reduce democracy as well. Economic security and political freedoms are always "positively correlated", as statisticians say. When freedom increases, so does economic security and vice versa.

Among the foremost responsibilities for those who want European progress are the defence of the European model and initiatives to improve it. In the first chapter, I tried to illustrate the elite's insatiable drive to accumulate ever greater wealth, a predisposition both the Constitution and the Reform Treaty support. Now we have come full-circle and – thanks to the ILO – we can measure what Europeans have accomplished through their struggles, within a democratic framework for which they have also had to fight.

The European Union, as it now exists, no longer provides this scope for democracy. Its institutions, in particular the Commission, undermine both economic and political security. Control of social policy supposedly "remains with" the Member States but these states find it difficult – supposing they even try – to resist the demands of their own elite and the pressures of the market.

The European Court of Justice aids and abets. Its jurisprudence, as far as a non-jurist understands it, accepts that competition rules do not apply to "basic" social protection, when and if it is compulsory. But any additional and/or optional social protection, even when supplied by non-profit organisations, is subject to the usual rules of "free and undistorted competition". In most European countries, the ECJ's decisions will have an impact on health, education and pensions. Jurists and lawyers, not citizens and their representatives will be making those decisions.

Let us give the last word to a wise European:

Yet a government truly of the people should make sure that they are not too poor because poverty undermines democracy... measures therefore should be taken to give them lasting prosperity; and as this is equally the interest of all classes, including the prosperous, the proceeds of the public revenues should be accumulated and distributed among the people of modest means, if possible enough to enable them to purchase some property or at least enough so that they can make a beginning in trade or husbandry.[4]

What a fine government we could have if Europe and Europeans, after 24 centuries, finally listened to Aristotle.

Conclusion

What is Europe, and who, exactly, are Europeans?

Europeans are a strange mixture, as they have proven over the centuries; both extraordinarily creative and incredibly dangerous. European history has given birth to inspiring periods like the Renaissance, the Reformation and the Enlightenment that led the way towards the liberation of the human spirit. The continent's cultural contributions are universally acknowledged. Europe invented Greek drama, opera, the symphony orchestra, easel painting; it evolved political institutions like parliamentary democracy, public trial by jury with rights for the defence; habeas corpus, universal suffrage and... Constitutions.

The social and political battles Europeans fought over the centuries, especially since the Enlightenment and the French Revolution, forged a culture, an identity and a social model found nowhere else on the globe – and set us apart from peoples who followed a different historical path.

But whatever their best, Europeans have also shown themselves capable of the worst. For hundreds of years, they asserted their power through imperialism, absolutism, and all-out war. The savagery of the Crusaders would have impressed even the Mongols.[1] Christianity profoundly influenced institutions, culture, and mindsets and it is curious to note, as the well-known French historian Jacques

Le Goff has observed, that the current borders of the EU-25, excluding Greece – correspond exactly to the frontiers of Roman Catholic Christianity in the Middle Ages – with its full quota of heretic-hunts, torture and witch-incinerations. Religion took some responsibility for the poor, the sick and the oppressed, but it also justified wars, pogroms, and mass expulsions, notably of Jews, even though Europe did belatedly manage to separate Church and State.

Beginning in the nineteenth century, Europeans durably colonised a great many Southern countries, waging awful colonial wars whenever they found it necessary to keep the natives subservient. Even now, the wounds of colonialism have not fully healed and the scars will be visible for a long time to come.[2] In the twentieth century, Europeans invented fascism, totalitarian communism, the Shoah, the concentration camp and the gulag.

Europeans did not invent slavery, but they made plenty of tidy profits from it. World War was another European speciality that decimated several generations obliged to follow arrogant, power-hungry heads of state and stupid, bloodthirsty generals. Europe provided a perfect environment for class conflict; many people devoted their lives to attempting to improve the lot of the industrial working class, even if the Industrial Revolution had positive aspects as well.

At the outset, the European Union was certainly a great invention, in the tradition of Europe's finest moments. People believed the Union's institutions would represent a kind of crowning achievement for social gains won over decades and would keep the peace, overcoming entrenched hatreds, age-old national rivalries, and the confrontation between the haves and have-nots. The Union was to be the embodiment of peace, democracy and social progress.

Now we see that this Europe too is moving backwards, not because of the No vote that revealed rather than triggered this trend, but because of choices made by the European leadership over the past two decades at least. The Union is regressing politically, socially and culturally. A majority of French and Dutch voters detected the dangers of regression inherent in the Constitution and rejected it.

True, the Yes–No fault-lines were ambiguous. No one denies that without the vote of the right-wing, the No could not have scored a 55 per cent victory in France and won more than 60 per cent in Holland. Still, even the fiercest and most vocal supporters of the Yes had to admit that the right was a small minority in the No camp. A few weeks into the French campaign, everyone tacitly recognised that hurling insults across the left–right divide served no purpose – because for every rightwing Le Pen supporter voting No, you could find a MEDEF member – or a Berlusconi or a Haider – rooting for the Yes.

The real division in my view was between those who favour an Americanised, competitive, neo-liberal model seen as more "efficient" and those who want to defend the European social model. The employers' union MEDEF welcomed anyone who voted Yes; the Socialist Party thought you could be neo-liberal and still save social Europe. Millions of people voted Yes because they felt that a No would be a rejection of the European idea itself, or out of fear that the No would drag Europe further down, and faster. Many of these people are potential allies in the fight for a Europe of the common good.

Now that the Constitution is history and the virtually identical Reform Treaty has replaced it, the confrontation will be between those who still want American-style neo-liberalism and social regression and those who hope that another No could finally make European elites and governments recognise that something is amiss. Instead of doggedly insisting on the same old policies, only worse, they might – if mightily pushed – be obliged to turn to the traditional European spirit of innovation, creativity, democracy and social progress rather than following the destructive tendencies that have so often triumphed in Europe's darkest past. In our own time, contempt for the weak, the religion of money, the acceptance of blatant inequality and the refusal to share – all hallmarks of modern, globalised capitalism – are every bit as barbarous as colonialism or slavery were in their day. If Europe gives in to these temptations, the result will be devastating for everyone, not just for the poor and vulnerable.

We have plenty of empirical evidence showing that the market and competition alone will never lead to full employment or to social inclusion for all. The American road has led to full-blown financial crisis, proving that the State has to be deeply involved in regulation. Neo-liberalism is a palpable failure. But we can only preserve, protect and enhance the European model if all Member States are willing to cooperate to achieve it. The Union in general and the Commission in particular have shown zero spontaneous willingness to lead in this direction and this reluctance can be blamed in the last analysis on the Member States themselves.

Our fight is to make our governments understand that they must make of Europe a truly twenty-first-century civilisation; that if they refuse, we shall collectively become a largely peripheral political failure, a mere American satellite, though with more grandiose historical monuments. People must take matters into their own hands and push their governments to change direction. To choose mediocrity today is to choose irrelevance.

The European Social Forum is one setting for contributing to this project – if it finally decides to be both social and European. To date, the ESF, like the World Social Forum, has dealt with myriad subjects but lacked defining goals. It radiates energy and goodwill; one can take great pleasure in being together but it has also given too much attention to non-European issues. Europeans have no chance of changing the world if they cannot first change Europe, nor solve the world's problems if they can't solve their own. Progressive Europeans must devote scarce time and resources to improving our own continent and to making Europeans responsible world citizens. Previous ESFs have sometimes contributed to creating or strengthening of networks – for example on public services – and these outcomes should be replicated in other areas. We now confront a political elite determined to lock up Europe in a permanent, high-security, neo-liberal detention centre and we must be equally determined to stop them, no matter how difficult the conditions we now confront.

None of this requires that anyone anywhere abandon their main "cause", whether it's trade, women's rights, tax havens, food sovereignty, climate change, trade union affairs, collusion in the American war... Diversity is beneficial and we face no shortage of injustices to combat. We can, however, give all of them a European dimension; setting objectives and obliging European politicians to define themselves in terms of these goals. We must also form better alliances, working with whoever agrees on that particular part of the agenda, even if this means in some instances accepting somewhat stranger bedfellows than we might otherwise do. Time is short.

Civil society can apply the principles of "variable geometry", or in political terms, enhanced cooperation, coming together in more or less sustained coalitions on selected issues, seeking out in each case as many partners in as many countries as we can find and trying to create a social dynamic.

We have great ancestors to remember and can draw strength from their courage. We have fine European progressive traditions for inspiration. We have the forces of intelligence, peace and progress, not always united, not always conscious of their own potential power, but present. We can, we must, build upon these foundations an authentically European future; otherwise the old demons will once again take over and lead us to mediocrity, or worse, to downfall. Every citizen has a voice and can play a part to escape such a fate. Every citizen can be present at the creation of a Europe for the common good. This must be our priority and our hope. Another Europe is possible.

Notes

1 The War on Society

1. Adam Smith, *The Wealth of Nations*, 1776, Book III, Chapter IV, p. 512 (ed. Andrew Skinner; London: Penguin, 1974).
2. Philippe Askenazy, CNRS and Cepremap. "Partage de la valeur ajoutée et rentabilité du capital en France et aux Etats-Unis: une réévaluation", *Economie Statistique*, nos. 363, 364 (2003).
3. Eurostat: Statistiques en bref; Gérard Abramovici, "La protection sociale en Europe", *Population et conditions sociales*, Thème 3 (2004).
4. Valéry Giscard d'Estaing interviewed by James Graff, *Time International*, 23 June 2003 (website posting dated 15 June 2003).
5. Many thanks to the authors of Attac's book on the TEC (*Cette "Constitution" qui piège l'Europe*, Paris: Mille et Une Nuits, 2005), who drew up a list of rights not mentioned or guaranteed by the Charter that do exist in the French Constitution of 1958 or in French law.
6. Stephen Castle, "Profile of VGE", *Independent on Sunday*, 1 June 2003. Olivier Duhamel's book *Pour l'Europe* (Paris: Le Seuil, 2003), which includes his "Journal d'un conventionnel" or "A Convention member's diary", is a mine of information about the story of the Convention.
7. Michael Leverson Meyer, "Is Europe broken?", *Newsweek International*, 12 August 2002. The American Constitution is only 5,000 words long, yet it has been applied since 1787.
8. UNICE, Treaty Establishing a European Constitution: Synthesis Note, no date.
9. Baron Daniel Janssen, "The pace of economic change in Europe", speech given to the General Assembly of the Trilateral Commission, Tokyo, April 2000.
10. Graff interview of Valéry Giscard d'Estaing.
11. See *Le Canard Enchaîné*, 30 March 2005, p. 3.

12. Castle, "Profile of VGE".
13. For a longer account of the GATS campaign, visit www.france. attac.org, "Campagnes" heading, then "AGCS" subheading.
14. Jean-Paul Fitoussi, *La politique de l'impuissance, Entretien avec Jean-Claude Guillebaud* (Paris: Arléa, 2005), p. 96.
15. Ibid., p. 92.

2   They Voted Yes, or Surviving on a Diet of Humble Pie

1. VGE is quoted in the newspaper *Le Parisien*, 18 March 2005.
2. Claudie Haigneré, "La Constitution mérite le débat", *Libération*, 25 March 2005.
3. All the quotes concerning social protection are derived from Articles III-209 and 210.
4. Olivier Duhamel, *Pour l'Europe* (Paris: Le Seuil, 2003), p. 58 ff. The deposit date of the French Socialist demands is not specified. Duhamel, who has a spot every weekday morning on France-Culture radio, was passionately in favour of the Yes and never let his listeners forget it.
5. Ibid., p. 61.
6. "Pour l'Europe: les exigences des socialistes", text of the SP central committee, adopted by the Socialist Party National Council on 11 October 2003.
7. Quoted in www.nouvelobs.com, 2 April 2005.
8. See Colin Williams, "The Treaty of Nice", *European Business Journal*, 22 December 2001.
9. Dominique Strauss-Kahn, president, *Building a Political Europe, 50 Proposals for the Europe of Tomorrow*. Report of the Roundtable established at the initiative of the president of the European Commission, April 2004.
10. John Blau, "Trans-Atlantic brain drain worries Europe's policy makers", *Research-Technology Management* (published by the Industrial Research Institute), 1 March 2004.
11. Strauss-Kahn, *Building a Political Europe*, conclusion.
12. Quoted in Janet Bush, "You don't understand the rules of the Eurogame? You'd be more worried if you did", *Independent on Sunday*, 27 February 2005.

13. Mandelson was speaking at a New Labour conference in June 2002, also attended by Bill Clinton. His contribution was published in *The Times* on 10 June 2002.

3 The Common Good: Towards an Alternative Europe

1. "EU founder member ratifies constitution", *Financial Times*, 11 July 2005.

4 Europe as a Geopolitical Power

1. See the dossier prepared for the press by the CED, 26 May 2005 and the site www.defense.gouv.fr/sites/CED, especially the section "Rôle".
2. "Europe warned to boost its weapons' spending or risk being left behind US", *Financial Times*, 6 June 2005.
3. The foreign minister of another EU country informed me (personal communication) that both these provisions had been included in the Constitution at the express request of France.
4. This quote and those that follow are from Robert Kagan's long article "Power and Weakness", *Policy Review*, no. 113, June 2002. Soon after, this article became a book, *Of Paradise and Power* (New York: Knopf, 2003).
5. CED Report 2005, Tables p. 382 ff.
6. China ranked third in total GNP and in terms of wealth per capita has attained an average $6,450, a figure that increases yearly due to China's spectacular growth rates. GNPs per capita are calculated in terms of "purchasing power parity" – PPP. This measure is now the norm for the World Bank, the IMF and the CIA. See www.cia.gov/cia/publications/factbook/.
7. David Harvey, *A Brief History of Neoliberalism* (Oxford and New York: Oxford University Press, 2005), quoting the work of Gérard Dumenil and Dominique Lévy, pp. 16–17.
8. In 2003, Japan's monetary reserves were $664 billion, China was next with $413 billion, Taiwan ($207 billion), South Korea ($155 billion), Hong Kong ($118 billion) and India ($103 billion). All these figures, particularly China's, have since grown.

9. United Nations (UNCTAD) *World Investment Report*, 2004.
10. I developed these aspects in *Another World is Possible If...* (London: Verso, 2004), chapter 5 so will not repeat myself here except to stress the importance of the European model in shaping a superpower Europe.

5   The Environmental Challenge

1. See Jeffrey McNeely and Sara Scherr, *Common Ground, Common Future: How Ecoagriculture Can Help to Feed the World and Save Wild Biodiversity* (IUCN Future Harvest, 2001).
2. C.D. Thomas and A. Cameron et al., "Extinction risk from climate change", *Nature*, no. 427, pp. 145–8, 8 January 2004.
3. IPCC, *Climate Change 2001*, Working Group 1: The Scientific Basis (UNEP–WMO–IPCC, 2001). IPCC has three working groups: WG1 deals with the scientific basis; WG2 with the probable impacts; WG3 with strategies to counter those impacts. Further reports reinforcing the 2001 conclusions have been published subsequently.
4. Robin McKie, "How we put the heat on nature", *Observer*, 1 February 2005, quoting Sir David King, chief scientific advisor to the British government.
5. *Millennium Ecosystem Assessment*, March 2005. See www.maweb.org.
6. "The edge of the abyss: Within ten years climate change will be irreversible, so why no action?", editorial, *New Scientist*, 26 March 2005, p. 5.
7. *Fragments: the Collected Wisdom of Heraclitus*, trans. Brooks Haxton (New York: Viking Penguin, 2001), Fragment no. 98.
8. Jared Diamond, *Collapse: How Societies Choose to Fail or Succeed* (New York: Viking, 2005).
9. M. Wackernagle and W. Rees, *Our Ecological Footprint* (Canada: New Society Publishers, 1996).
10. Richard Wray, "BP fails to reduce greenhouse gases", *Guardian*, 12 April 2005. BP still does better than its American rival Exxon, whose CO_2 emission in 2005 reached 135 million tonnes.
11. George Monbiot, "An agricultural crime against humanity", *Guardian*, 6 November 2007.

6 Social Insecurity

1. International Labour Organisation, International Labour Office, Socio-Economic Security Programme, *Economic Security for a Better World* (Geneva, 2004). This 450-page report will not be put online. It is fairly expensive (50 Swiss francs), available only in English and virtually unobtainable except through the ILO itself. Despite all this, it is worth making the effort to obtain it (particularly libraries). Go to pubvente@ilo.org or directly to the SES programme: ses@ilo.org.
2. See the list in the above report, p. 40.
3. Gérard Filoche, *Democracie et Socialisme*, 5 July 2005, my translation.
4. Aristotle, *The Politics*, my adaptation from the Garnier-Flammarion French edition, 1993, Book VI, chapter 5.

Conclusion

1. As Amin Maalouf has shown in his admirable book *Les Croisades vues par les Arabes* (Paris: Lattès, 1983).
2. The relationship between European achievements and European colonialism and plunder, and the contribution of the latter to the former, cannot be dealt with here.

Index

Compiled by Sue Carlton